ROBERT SOMMER, author of this book, is Professor of Psychology and Chairman of the Psychology Department at the University of California at Davis. He is the author of numerous articles on the effects of physical setting upon attitudes and behavior.

Personal Space

The Behavioral Basis of Design

Personal Space

The Behavioral Basis of Design

Robert Sommer

Prentice-Hall, Inc. *Englewood Cliffs, N. J.*

Preface

Knowledge about man's immediate environment, the hollows within his shelters that he calls offices, classrooms, corridors, and hospital wards, is as important as knowledge about outer space and undersea life. For too long we have accepted physical forms and administrative arrangements based upon outdated views of human activity. We are told that classrooms should have straight rows of chairs so the children will face the teacher, prisoners should be kept in separate jail cells, college students should have roommates, and park benches should be heavy and indestructible so that vandals will not cart them away. With or without a conscious philosophy or explicit recognition of the fact, designers are shaping people as well as buildings. Over the last ten years I have been involved in numerous design projects in one capacity or another. For the most part I have been asked the wrong questions— i.e., "What are the proper dimensions of a prison cell?" In one sense, the question is logical. It is possible to determine the size and shape preferred by prisoners and guards, the best sort of lighting, the optimal distance between bars, the colors most suitable for prison walls, and whether carpeting is sufficiently durable for cell interiors. There is a double irony in the situation—first, that such questions are asked so rarely, and second, that they ignore the superordinate questions about prisons as they relate to society's goals. If prisons fail to rehabilitate convicts, I doubt that it is because the walls are grey rather than blue or the bars six inches apart rather than eight.

An architect is in an impossible situation, a plight he shares with educators, physicians, and lawyers. Perhaps his situation is a little more impossible in that he must supervise, collaborate, or adapt his activity to accord with the demands of an almost limitless array of professionals, technicians, and government officials, but the difference is in degree and not quality. There is no guarantee that design professionals—city planners, landscape designers, architects, interior designers, and industrial designers—would benefit from college courses in sociology, but I have no doubt that they would gain by adopting a functionalism based on user behavior as a guiding principle. This does not mean that the customer is always right or *vox populi, vox dei,* but only that some effort should be made to see how satisfactory a building is from the standpoint of the different publics involved. The term *user* is employed here in the broad sense of all the people involved with a structure. It should not be possible to write a textbook about design that omits consideration of user behavior. The title of this book, *Personal Space,* reflects two usages of the term. The first refers to the emotionally charged zone around each person, sometimes described as a soap bubble or aura, which helps to regulate the spacing of individuals. The second usage refers to the processes by which people mark out and personalize the spaces they inhabit.

Several of the studies described in this book were aided by grants from the U.S. Office of Education. I am indebted to Nancy Russo and Peter Klopfer for their comments on the manuscript and to Margaret Hill and Peggy Todd for secretarial assistance. For many of the ideas in this book, I owe major intellectual debts to Humphrey Osmond, Sim van der Ryn, Glen McBride, Peter Klopfer, Edward Hall, and Erving Goffman. My wife, Dorothy, and our children bore patiently the years of research, writing, and editing that produced this book.

Contents

PART ONE
Spatial Behavior

PART TWO
Special Settings

List of Figures and Tables

Figures

Tables

Personal Space

The Behavioral Basis of Design

PART ONE

Spatial Behavior

1

Values in the Design Process—

The Axiology of Space

More and more homeowners, it seems, are fencing themselves in. A Boston fence maker estimates his sales are rising at the rate of 45 per cent a year, while his counterparts in Washington describe their business as "fantastic." In Houston's yellow pages, no fewer than 47 fence companies currently advertise their wares, ranging from waist high chain links to six-foot cedars. (*Newsweek,* November 7, 1966)

We are now in the midst of reshaping the environment on an unprecedented scale, but we do not know what we are doing to ourselves. The design professions ranging from interior decorators concerned with single offices to regional planners concerned with entire river valleys are involved to varying degrees. Occasionally, as with Oscar Niemeyer and Brasilia, they have a central role, but all too often the designers are consulted too late and asked the wrong questions. Frank Lloyd Wright put forth the doctrine that form follows function, which became a useful antidote to needless ornamentation. Yet it is curious that most of the concern with functionalism has been focused upon form rather than function. It is as if the structure itself—harmony with the site, the integrity of the materials, the cohesiveness of the separate units, has become the function. Relatively little emphasis is placed on the activities taking place inside the structure. This is predictable in the case of the architect who, in his training and practice, learns to look at buildings without people in them. Lavishly colored photographs in glossy magazines show empty rooms and corridors, tables fully set with plates, silverware, and wine glasses, an open book on the sofa, and a fire burning in the hearth but not a sign of people anywhere.

It is also common to find lavish descriptions of buildings before they are opened for use. I had occasion to visit the prototype "flexible school," a building shell whose internal dimensions can be altered quickly and inexpensively through the use of demountable wall partitions. Thousands of educators had visited the model and read the well-illustrated pamphlets describing the building. Unfortunately, the group of architects and educators who developed the prototype was disbanded even before the first school patterned along the lines of the model opened its doors. The model itself was to be used for other purposes. I am not criticizing this project specifically, for what is involved is standard practice in architecture. A recent issue of *College Management* described how Wisconsin State University at Stephens Point saved a great deal of money by remodeling a dormitory with smaller furniture so that a third occupant could be added to each double room. I have no objection to the idea in theory, but it would be nice to know how this affected the students. The same phenomenon occurs in city planning, too. It was not until I was three-quarters through a glowing account of the New Town of Columbia, Maryland that I realized the ground had been broken only recently, and it would be years before the site resembled a town. I have no argument with planning a city before it is built—that seems the logical time to plan it—but rhapsodic accounts of how it will work in practice are likely, particularly if they are written by prominent architects and planners, to outlive the city. The activities, population, and economic base of the community may change completely, but people outside will know New Town from its preconstruction plans and models.

What is needed is a shift in temporal perspective. Just as scientists are thinking more about the future, designers must shift some of their attention away from the past (buildings that have been) and the future (Utopias) and study buildings on the narrow plane of the present and from the standpoint of user behavior. Individual practitioners must abandon the philosophy of "never look back." In many cases there is ample money for a library committee or school board to spend several years visiting comparable facilities when they are planning a new building. Occasionally they may go to Europe to see what is happening there. Yet there will be no money for follow-up studies of the building in action. Once the structure is opened for public use, the architect disappears from the scene.

The doctrine that architecture can be conceived of as great hollow sculpture or timeless unchanging form whose existence is an end in itself must be discarded. Architecture may be beautiful, but it should be more than that; it must enclose space in which certain activities can take place comfortably and efficiently. Not only must form follow function, but it must assist it in every way. The personal expression of the architect must yield to the functions that the building serves. It is possible to imagine a different situation where architects would be primarily artists given free rein to enclose certain spaces beautifully. Someone else would be charged with the task of finding uses for the hollows within the sculpture—a committee would decide that this hollow would make a good factory, that one a courtroom, and the small one over here a suitable private home for a retired couple. Although the situation sounds improbable, it is the ordinary state of affairs in basic science. A man applies for $50,000 to study iron oxides or plankton, and it is up to others, primarily applied scientists, engineers, and commercial firms, to determine how the results may be utilized. At the moment, however, architecture remains an applied discipline, and the architect plans structures to meet his clients' needs.

An alternative to a functionalism based on user behavior and satisfaction is to use symmetry, cohesiveness, or landscape fittingness as absolute values. These are not only highly subjective, but they also place undue emphasis on external appearance. They have encouraged the development of an extensive self-congratulation system within the design professions. Rarely are design awards based on the experiences of the building's users, or even a site visit by the busy panel members, but on the basis of glossy photographs. Reform of the panel system seems less important than the question of what criteria the jury uses to evaluate buildings. The present system is reasonable if architects are giving themselves awards for sculpture, but not if the awards are intended for buildings in which certain activities will take place.

The visual thinking of the architect contrasts greatly with the abstract analytical thinking of the social scientist, philosopher, and most laymen and represents a serious impediment to fruitful dialogue between them. Architects use words to drape around pictures, but the layman sits waiting for a message that will be exemplified or illustrated by the pictures. This makes it extraordinarily difficult to preach to architects through words alone, a fact recognized by most design periodicals ("glossies"), which are known for their lavish illustrations and inane texts. On several occasions I was surprised to find design editors removing statistical tables from articles I had submitted and requesting photographs instead. This makes sense to me now, and whenever I discuss a topic with designers, e.g., dormitories or airport waiting rooms, I generally have several eight by ten glossy prints with me.

The stage that each design profession has reached can be measured along a scale from pure artistry at one end to pure scientism at the other. Closest to the artistic end are the interior designers who operate mainly on a pre-empirical intuitive level. The notion of Period Design relies on historical research of a sort, but the net effect is one of copying or weaving elements into a coherent pattern without attempting to evaluate the effects of different arrangements. Architecture is somewhat further along in that it is an empirical art, relying heavily on the accumulation of experience with different building types. When it comes to materials and structures, architects join engineers in carrying out systematic research, but in the behavioral realm, the way buildings affect people, architects fall back on intuition, anecdote, and casual observation. Consultants flourish in the design fields because there is no body of information assembled in such a way that it is useful to architects and other design professionals. Hence the tremendous importance of library consultants, church consultants, hospital consultants—all experts by experience, older men and women whose ideas may be behind the times.

The modern architectural firm is a bureaucratic monster designed to cope with the other bureaucracies—corporate as well as governmental—with whom it must deal. At the heart of an architectural giant is a computer surrounded by departments of architectural systems, structures, mechanical systems, electrical systems, urban systems, and research. One step removed from this are the Category Teams dealing with commercial buildings, educational buildings, health buildings, public housing, and so forth. These are the real design groups who develop the specifications for each category of building. Their findings are used by the specific project teams working on individual jobs. As men concerned with the application of knowledge and technique, architects have usually worked in teams. In the past the teams could be small, consisting of an architect and a few skilled workmen. Now the teams can be extraordinarily large and will include a design group, structures people, sales specialists, sewage system analysts, town planners, as well as economists, sociologists, and environmental biologists. With the increasing number of specialists in the design process, communication problems multiply. Many architects who have joined large construction firms or investment houses are indistinguishable from other corporation employees.

Even the hallowed blueprints are on the way out. In five years' time, all computations and visual representations may be done by the computer. The 1,100 sheets of drawings that went into the design of the Chicago Civic Center Court Building and cluttered the architect's office for almost a year will be a thing of the past. Such massive accumulations of paper frequently produced an unseemly rush to "finish the project and get the drawings out of the office!"

The architect's *bête noire* is the builder, who may be seen as the un-professional and unscrupulous fellow who builds houses without archi-tects from designs drawn on the backs of envelopes. There is also a great deal of rivalry within the other design professions. Engineers criticize architects for an overconcern with esthetic values and a ne-glect of function and efficiency. Interior designers accuse architects of trying to dominate the design field and doing them out of their com-missions on purchases. Landscape architects resent being called in last on a job to apply the green paint. There is great fear that non-professionals affiliated with large companies will come to dominate the entire design field. Architects criticize nonarchitect-designed homes estimated to constitute 90 per cent of the market. Planners lament the expediency of elected officials who discard years of planning to satisfy an influential land developer or business firm. All too often the gas station or power line goes where the company wants it and the plan goes back into the files. Interior designers battle valiantly against incursions of furniture manufacturers and wholesale distributors into their domain. Independent landscape architects take a dim view of the greenery manufacturers who market their wares directly to an unsuspecting public. Nor are landscape architects very happy about the role of engineers in the planning process. This conflict was clear in the recent resignation of Lawrence Halprin as landscape architect for the Bay Area Rapid Transit. Halprin complained that he was never asked the right questions about anything important. The cor-ridor for the transit system had already been selected, and matters such as placing it underground or above ground or using under-passes versus overpasses were regarded as policy decisions outside the scope of the design consultants. The engineers apologetically explained that they didn't have any money for mosaic tiles in the train stations or for fountains in the plaza, but Halprin wasn't interested in these things—he wanted to discuss rights-of-way, the effects of an elevated system on the surrounding community, and the need for pedestrian routes over the right-of-way.

This is not intended to be a book for architects, designers, or city planners as such, even though several chapters are aimed more or less in their direction. All people are builders, creators, molders, and shapers of the environment; we are the environment. The specialized design fields see themselves helpless in the face of massive problems on every side. The day when society can call upon the architect-priest or the scientist-priest or the psychoanalyst-priest to solve its major ills has passed. Society needs the talents of the gamut of specialized and unspecialized professions centered around human survival and welfare. Within these groups there is an intense realization that over-specialization in a changing world is a sure prescription for failure. Across the nation, schools of architecture and design are becoming institutes of environmental planning, environmental science, design science, and environmental engineering. At the moment the change is more evident on paper than in curriculum, but it is coming.

Much has been written about behavioral science as a tool for regimentation and thought control. There has been less discussion of the ways that social science can free men from misconceptions and strengthen individuality in an increasingly conformist society. The Kinsey report has had a profound effect upon discussions of human sexual behavior. It would be an exaggeration to say that it has produced the so-called sexual revolution, but there is no question that people can discuss homosexuality, adultery, and premarital intercourse in a more meaningful and concrete way now. We do not have to accept the Kinsey statistics as precise or immutable to gain considerable knowledge from the reports. Kinsey helped dispel some of the fog and confusion surrounding sexual behavior by using terms in an unemotional and consistent way, which has enabled later workers, psychologists as well as zoologists, to ask meaningful questions and undertake experimental work that would have been inconceivable 25 years ago.[1]

As with research into sexual behavior, environmental studies have not followed any over-all plan; they have proceeded in fits and starts depending upon local interest and the availability of funds. The concern of the 1900's with the esthetics of color shifted as interest in pure philosophy waned to the functional aspects of color in homes and factories, and finally, in the era of the doctor-priest, to the therapeutic prescription of color. Investigators have displayed great ingenuity in locating funds for environmental studies. The Bell Telephone Company has supported work on communications flow through spatial networks; civil defense people have underwritten studies of crowding; the Navy has backed some very fine work on group processes in confinement; the Ford Foundation supports studies of community development, and the Department of Interior is concerned with recreation and resources management. Many large corporations have supported basic research into people's reactions to light, sound, and color patterns. Under the heading of human engineering or ergonomics, they have also supported applied studies of carpeting in hospitals and schools, background music in stores and offices, and the legibility of highway road

[1] Alfred C. Kinsey et al., *Sexual Behavior in the Human Male* (Philadelphia: W. B. Saunders Co., 1948).

signs. A landmark in this sort of work is the recent publication of the volume *The Bathroom: Criteria for Design*[2] summarizing eight years of work undertaken by Cornell authorities and supported largely by plumbing supplies.

Our book represents an attempt to elucidate some of the questions of value involved in the design process in which matters of physical form arise only after one has decided what he wants to do. As the chapter title suggests ("axiology" is the study of values), design questions involve value judgments—most specifically, whose values are to be served? The term "building program" is a misnomer for a preliminary analysis that should be more philosophical than technical, a statement of purpose rather than a list of hardware.

The clearest realization of the connection between environmental form and human behavior is taking place in the institutional field. People trained in hospital administration, education, and business management are aware of the important contributions research and development have made in most aspects of their work. They are surprised to find that decisions regarding the physical plant amounting to tens of millions of dollars are made without adequate information about user behavior. Whether it is a matter of separate or bunk beds in college dormitories, secluded or exposed nurses' stations in hospitals, open or partitioned offices, ceilings eight or eight-and-one-half feet in apartments, it is evident that little is known as to how the alternatives affect people. One of the best descriptions of the problem is found in an article about school furniture by the educator L. K. Pinnell who interviewed teachers, principals, pupils, custodians, and furniture manufacturers. At any given moment, he felt, superintendents, business managers, and purchasing agents were sitting down with salesmen and arranging the purchase of school desks, classroom teachers in other schools were evaluating their own furniture and making recommendations to their own administrators, custodians were cleaning and moving furniture, muttering to themselves and the maintenance engineer about the problems they encountered, pupils were telling one another or their parents whether or not they were pleased with their new desks, and all this went on while furniture manufacturers decried their lack of information on how furniture fit into an educational program. Collectively, Pinnell believes, these various parties possess all the information available regarding school seating, but each group is unfamiliar with the information possessed by the others.[3] Teachers lack

[2] Alexander Kira, *The Bathroom: Criteria for Design* (New York: Bantam Books, Inc., 1966).

[3] L. K. Pinnell, *Functionality of Elementary School Desks*, Bureau of Laboratory Schools Publication No. 5. (Austin: University of Texas Press, 1954).

information about the furniture that is available and often are not consulted when it comes to purchases; business managers are removed from the classroom situation and often evaluate furniture largely on the basis of cost, style, and a good sales talk.

Designing functional areas or multipurpose space does not complete the architect's task. It is equally important to show the residents how to use the space productively and to develop effective institutional policies governing space allocation and utilization. A man who is assigned a large work area may use it less efficiently than someone assigned half the area. This is related to life style since some people will accommodate themselves to anything, no matter how uncomfortable or dysfunctional, either because they do not know how to improve the situation or believe that rules forbid them to alter the arrangement. This is especially likely to happen in institutional architecture where space is occupied by nonowners for short periods. How many people significantly alter the chairs in an airport terminal or a doctor's waiting room? It is a matter of intimidation, inertia, and the belief that results do not warrant extra effort. People accept the idea that the existing arrangement is justified according to some mysterious principle known only to the space owners—Dr. X must have some reason for placing his chairs so close together, and the store owner must have some logical purpose for putting the shopping carts in front of the magazine rack. It frequently happens that the chief enforcers of spatial norms are the janitors and maintenance employees. It may be asking a great deal of an architect, but he must be sensitive to the intimate connections between spatial norms, bureaucracy, and the functions of a building. It is exceedingly likely that, should he return for a visit after the building has been in use, there will be two sales managers in the offices he designed for one, and 40 pupils in the classroom he designed for 30.

This book is divided into two parts; the first an introduction to spatial behavior and the second an application of these concepts to particular settings. Chapters 2 to 6 will describe various mechanisms for controlling the distribution and density of people, the methods that have been evolved to keep people out of one another's way. This will include dominance relationships in which a person knows where he belongs socially, and territoriality, his knowledge of his spatial place. We will discuss the intimate connection between space and status and then explore what is meant by privacy. Despite the large numbers of people around, we simply are not bumping into one another. Various conventions and rules have been developed to complement architectural forms in keeping people out of one another's way. Although we will discuss research with animals as well as humans, there is no implication that the underlying mechanisms are the same in both cases.

The second part of the book is devoted to certain man-environment systems ranging from schools to old folks' homes considered from the standpoint of user behavior. These examples are mainly for illustrative purposes, to show methods and their applications, rather than for their substantive findings. I believe that social sciences make their greatest contribution by offering methods by which information about human behavior can be objectively and validly obtained, rather than formulating detailed laws about people's responses to blue walls, round buildings, or thatched roofs. People live and multiply in the frigid Arctic, Near East deserts, African rain forests, and the megalopolis of the eastern seaboard. People's needs are neither rigidly fixed nor infinitely varied. There is a price to be paid for every environmental adaptation, and frequently that price is the disappearance of species members who could not make the change. When we speak of *user behavior* we do not mean some hypothetical adaptation of which some humans somewhere may be capable, but rather the behavior of the immediate or prospective occupants. We will turn our attention now to the spatial accommodations of people in face-to-face groups.

2

The Alpha Animal

Wherever McDonald sits, there is the head of the table.

It is interesting that more is known about animal than about human spatial behavior. Zoologists and ecologists are concerned with species in the field; zookeepers, circus managers, and animal breeders have amassed a significant body of information about the proper conditions for captive animals. We know, for example, the connection between crowding of chickens and egg-laying and the spacing of cows at the trough and food consumption. If a captive animal is given too little, too much, or the wrong kind of space, it is likely to become ill, lose its body sheen, fail to reproduce, and eventually die. Since zoo animals are expensive, this is sufficient reason to undertake research into conditions necessary for their survival. Much work has gone into the ways animals adapt to shared space. Two of the most important concepts to emerge from this work are *territoriality* and *dominance behavior*. Both processes limit aggression because an individual either refrains from going where he is likely to be involved in disputes or, based on his knowledge of who is above and below him, to engage in ritualized dominance-subordination behavior rather than in actual combat.

The complementary relationship between territoriality and dominance behavior is expressed in Victor Hugo's declaration, "Every man a property owner, no one a master." The implication is that when everyone possesses an individual territory, the reasons for one man to dominate another disappear. Unlike most forms of social organization,

12

which tend to weaken or disappear in captivity, dominance relationships in captivity are often strengthened or even created where none existed previously.[1] A herd of deer whose natural food is scattered over fields will not fight over food as it grazes, but if the deer are fed grain in a small area so that the animals get in each other's way, they soon establish a dominance order in which the strongest animals have readiest access to food. Dominance orders among penned chickens may be linear or there may be pecking triangles. In groups with males and females, the males usually show passive dominance over females with each sex having its own peck order. Among young chickens a peck order is formed between the tenth and twelfth weeks. Once a dominance order is formed, a newcomer is at a disadvantage since he must engage in an encounter with each of the residents. In a comparison of flocks some of which had been together for a long time and others kept in flux by the regular rotation of birds, there was greater social stress and more overt aggression among the alternated birds. The stable group consumed more food, maintained or gained body weight, and laid more eggs.[2]

Confinement studies of humans disclose many dominance phenomena. Examining the records of all aggressive acts between mental patients, Esser was able to discern a relatively stable dominance hierarchy. Replacements of patients as well as staff temporarily increase the number of aggressive acts and dominance displays. Changes in medication as well as clinical symptoms will move a patient up or down within the hierarchy.[3] Altman and Haythorn studied pairs of sailors in confinement where the individuals gradually withdrew from one another or "cocooned" so that each person rigorously respected the zone of personal space around his neighbor. Pairs that were incompatible in terms of dominance, both sailors either very high or very low so that no easy accommodation was possible, adhered more rigorously to preferences for a particular bed, table, or chair.[4] If we accept the authors' operational definition of territoriality (the consistent use of particular beds, chairs, and table areas), there is an interesting parallel to the animal studies, which show that both territoriality and dominance behavior are ways of maintaining a social order, and when one system cannot function, the other takes over.

[1] John P. Scott, *Animal Behavior* (Chicago: University of Chicago Press, 1958).

[2] A. M. Guhl, "Sociobiology and Man," *Bulletin of the Atomic Scientists* (October 1965), pp. 22–24.

[3] A. H. Esser *et al.*, "Territoriality of Patients on a Research Ward," *Recent Advances in Biological Psychiatry*, ed. J. Wortis, Volume 8 (New York: Plenum Press, 1965).

[4] Irving Altman and W. W. Haythorn, "The Ecology of Isolated Groups," *Behavioral Science*, XII (1967), 169–82.

With pairs incompatible in dominance, such as two highly dominant individuals, no stable order can be found, so aggression is limited by strict adherence to territorial rights.[5]

Scientists studying the social behavior of monkeys have placed pairs of animals in small test cages for a few minutes and allowed them to compete for pieces of food. The winner of the single encounter, or of the majority of encounters if there were several, was by definition the dominant animal. This test has been used to study the *home cage effect* by pairing monkeys sometimes in the cage of one animal, and sometimes in the cage of the other. In one study the dominance order among 28 possible pairs of animals was ascertained on neutral ground over a seven-day period. When the monkeys were later tested for dominance both as hosts in their own cages and as guests in another monkey's cage, it was found that the originally dominant monkey obtained upwards of 96 per cent of the food as host, but this was reduced to 62 per cent as guest. There was a dominance reversal in nine instances with the originally dominant animal obtaining less food than his previously subordinate host.

Baseball coaches and players are aware of the advantage given to a team playing in its own stadium. It is not only the presence of the hometown fans that makes the difference, but also a player's intimate knowledge of the special characteristics of the environment—every little mound on the diamond, the height and location of fences and guardrails, the likelihood of hitting home runs, and so on. Minnesota Fats, the poolhall genius, emphasized how a man had to be a real expert to travel from town to town and still win: "You really have to be a good player to beat a man in his hometown. Every table is different. The rubber is just like a person, it dies a little each year." [6]

With certain types of monkeys who have group territories, a clear differentiation can be made between the social purposes of dominance relationships and territoriality. Group territories keep individual groups apart and thereby preserve the integrity of the troop, whereas dominance is the basis for intragroup relationships. This provides a reasonable model for various non-Western human societies where land is owned communally and a status order regulates social intercourse.

[5] The term "territory" is used in the descriptive sense only. There is no implication that the behavior described is innate rather than learned or that the underlying mechanisms in studies with humans are similar to those described in studies of other species. Following Hediger I use the term to represent an area "which is first rendered distinctive by its owner in a particular way and, secondly, is defended by the owner." The major components of this definition are *personalization* and *defense*. See Henri Hediger, *Wild Animals in Captivity* (London: Butterworth & Co. [Publishers] Ltd., 1950).

[6] Interview with Minnesota Fats. Radio Station KPFA, Berkeley, July 22, 1965.

Western man uses a complex amalgam of individual ownership, communal ownership, and status relationship to maintain a social order. Perhaps the most unusual feature of human territories is the prevalence of "rented space," areas that belong to one person but are used by another for a prescribed period in return for a fee.

Group territoriality is expressed in national and local boundaries, a segregation into defined areas that reduces conflict. Segregation that is forced on one group by another has many undesirable consequences in stigmatizing members of the former, but it is one form of accommodation between two groups. Among the Swedes and Italians in the Lake Erie community studied by Mack, the early conflict that had arisen out of differences in language, religion, general cultural background and out of competition for jobs and space had not been replaced, even thirty years later, by cooperation. Rather, the conflict had been accommodated through residential and occupational segregation.[7] Similarly, the invisible border between black and white areas of Chicago's Ashland Avenue was graphically described by Gene Marine, a free-lance journalist.

> Sixty-third from Justine to Ashland is any ghetto block in America. Sammy's Lounge, three doors from Ashland, screams the presence of a three-piece rhythm and blues group; across the street an unnamed overheated restaurant sells links and ribs. There is a store front church, a liquor store with more wine than whiskey in the window, a beauty salon with a heavy traffic in wigs. On a humid late afternoon in August, people —black people—stroll aimlessly or stand idly in little knots.
>
> The next block, from Ashland to Marchfield, is equally typical. Three bars all bear the proud names of Irishmen. Teen-age blond girls pore avidly over an enormous selection of rock-and-roll and hairdo magazines in the drugstore. A brightly lit, airconditioned coffee shop offers ham and eggs at a bargain price until 11 a.m. In that block, too, people—white people—stand or stroll.[8]

On the sidewalk west of Ashland there was not one black, on the east side, not one white. All this was accomplished without a Berlin wall, a freeway, or railroad tracks, but by an invisible boundary that was accepted so naturally that no one glanced at it. In New York City the boundary is at 96th Street:

> The street is nothing less, you say, than Manhattan's Berlin wall. You stare across it as you stare over the wire at checkpoint Charlie into East

[7] Raymond W. Mack, "Ecological Patterns in an Industrial Shop," *Social Forces*, XXXII (1954), 351–56.

[8] Gene Marine, "I've Got Nothing Against the Colored, Understand," *Ramparts* (November 1966), p. 14.

Berlin, into another dispensation. You are staring into the Caribbean and Africa. You stand on wealthy ground staring at poverty; and wealth and poverty have this in common: the first sight of them is frightening.[9]

Except on rare occasions, the white gangs stay on their side of the line, and the black gangs stay on theirs. There is no question but that this segregation, in the short run at least, reduces overt intergroup conflict. I do not condone residential segregation any more than death or poverty, but it has certain social consequences and one of these is the reduction of overt conflict between members of different groups. The worst race riots have not occurred in the rigidly segregated areas of the South, but in the border or fringe areas of the North. I hasten to add that the solution to intergroup conflict does not lie in a stricter residential segregation, since the form and nature of the economy compels diverse individuals to come together with ever-increasing frequency—ghetto walls are crumbling around the world—but rather in the removal of the conditions that lead to intergroup conflict. When children are loudly pummeling one another over some toy or the last apple, the best short-run solution is to separate the combatants before the entire house is disrupted, but the only way to ensure future tranquility is to change the conditions that created the conflict. Segregation, whether voluntary or compulsory from the standpoint of the isolated group, is very much in evidence throughout the world today. Within American society there are discernible trends toward age being added to income and ethnic affiliation as criteria for segregation. The market for specialized (segregated) housing for young unmarried people is booming in southern California. The builders see themselves as being in the forefront of a major housing trend for apartments and recreational facilities for people of the same age groups with the same social interests. The most extreme example of self-segregation is found among the Utopians, who will be discussed in a later chapter.

Apart from societies with clear and enforced caste lines and military organizations (which do not really qualify as societies, although one can find microcosms of societies within them), the clearest dominance orders are found in closed communities with restricted movement and limited space. Within prison society, for example, not only lower bunks and soft prison jobs but certain cells are regarded as more desirable than others and become sources of contention within the inmate society. When the convict order becomes stabilized to the point where each person knows his place (both socially and spatially), dissension ends. In the Russian prison described by Dostoevsky, class dis-

[9] V. S. Pritchett, *New York Proclaimed* (New York: Harcourt, Brace & World, Inc., 1964), p. 90.

tinctions were rigidly observed. Like all prisoners with money, Dostoevsky had a convict cook and servant and purchased his own food, tea, and vodka.[10] However, in American prisons the constant turnover among inmates, particularly the addition of fresh fish of unknown rank, produces an atmosphere of constant tension that requires continuous venting in profanity and aggressive fantasy. Periodic riots and rebellions indicate the breakdown of a stable convict social system and the failure of traditional understandings between guards and convicts. Turnover among guards also produces the same probing for strength and weakness that occurs with a new fish. All residents of the cell block, convicts and guards alike, must wait until the new man (guard or convict) learns how thing really happen as distinct from the regulations. Guards delegate to the inmate leaders the authority over certain areas of inmate life in return for the convicts' maintaining order within their own group. A convict who steps out of bounds will usually by kept in check by other convicts long before he becomes a serious problem to the guards.

Because social and spatial orders serve similar functions, it is not surprising to find spatial correlates of status levels and, conversely, social correlates of spatial positions. In the barnyard the top chickens have the greatest freedom of space and can walk anywhere, whereas lower birds are restricted to small areas and can be pecked by other birds whereover they go.[11] Such trends are most marked at the food trough where, with space in short supply, dominant animals do not hesitate to push away subordinates. This process, which results in the subordinate animals receiving the least amount of food, has led ecologists to state that the *spatial distribution* of food, as well as the total quantity, must be considered when studying food as a factor in the ecology of a species. In human society the social elite possess more space in the form of larger homesites, more rooms per house, and vacation homes. In addition, they have greater spatial mobility and more opportunities to escape when they become tense, uncomfortable, or bored.

Status is expressed physically in ways of behaving as well as status symbols which are used (a) to indicate status, (b) to reinforce status, and (c) as requirements to insure the perpetuation of the existing status system. Status symbols permit a newcomer to know who is top dog at first glance. One can visit a town and see where the "best people" live. These symbols also reinforce the status of the recipient by providing him with more amenities, mobility, and access to in-

---

[10] F. Dostoevsky, *The House of the Dead* (New York: Grove Press, Inc., 1959).

[11] Glen McBride, *A General Theory of Social Organization and Behaviour* (St. Lucia: University of Queensland Press, 1964).

formation. To have the judge sitting above the jury not only indicates his status but reinforces it. Finally such symbols become codified into laws and customs that perpetuate the status system. To require that houses in a particular suburb cost a minimum of $25,000 and the lots exceed a large minimum size will keep out people below a certain income level. One government report described the large-lot requirement as "the symbol of a community anti-Negro policy." [12]

In many species the dominant animal has a territory which is larger and more desirable than that of other species members.[13] The same pressures operate in social situations where there is competition for any item in short supply. When one college was confronted with overflow enrollment's, there were frequently more students than available seats. The result was that the students of lower status—freshmen, sophomores, and those on probation—were dispossessed. The practice created a homeless aggregation of low-status students wandering from English to history to philosophy classes trying to gain admission.

There is also a connection between dominance and individual distance that was nicely illustrated in a study by King. After establishing the dominance relationship between pairs of chickens, he placed the dominant bird at the end of a runway with one foot tied to the floor, and then placed the subordinate bird at the other end of the runway. The distance a subordinate remained from the stationary dominant bird was linearly related to the frequency with which the dominant had pecked the subordinate in the home coop—that is, birds that had been pecked more remained further away. The experimenter was able to reduce approach distance to zero by rquiring the subordinate to approach the dominant to obtain food.[14] He later undertook an analogous study with children with similar results.[15]

Staehelin states that the amount of aggression shown by a patient in a mental hospital ward to an intruder depends on the dominance relationship between the two individuals. If the intruder is of higher rank, the patient is likely to take flight, but if the intruder is subordinate, the incumbent will stage an impressive display. Patients who were beaten most frequently were those who were physically the weakest, and had "the weakest personalities." [16] This suggests that domi-

[12] "Zoning Laws Conflict with Housing Aims," *Sacramento Bee*, May 19, 1968, p. C3.

[13] V. C. Wynne-Edwards, *Animal Dispersion in Relation to Social Behaviour* (Edinburgh: Oliver and Boyd, 1962).

[14] Murray G. King, "Peck Frequency and Minimal Approach Distance in Domestic Fowl," *Journal of Genetic Psychology*, CVI (1965), 25–28.

[15] ———, "Interpersonal Relations in Preschool Children and Average Approach Distance," *Journal of Genetic Psychology*, CIX (1966), 109–16.

[16] B. Staehelin, "Soziale Gesetzmäszigkeiten im Gemeinschaftsleben Geisteskranker." *Homo*, V (1954), 113–16.

nance relationships influence the intensity of the reaction to an invasion as well as whose space is likely to be invaded.

An institutionalized status hierarchy such as that found in armies or corporations is accompanied by complex spatial norms. There are many places where a factory supervisor cannot go without the workers feeling he is spying on them. Officers keep out of the enlisted men's quarters except on inspection. School administrators stay out of classrooms unless there is some emergency or a teacher asks them to visit. Whyte describes the dilemma of the restaurant supervisor who knows that problems exist in a given area but cannot go there because of status considerations without creating further problems.

> In the heat of the rush hour, we have seen pantry supervisors running up and down stairs, trying to get orders, trying to find out what is holding up things in the kitchen. Since they have supervisor status, the kitchen workers do not resist them openly, but the invasion of an upstairs supervisor tends to disrupt relations in the kitchen. It adds to the pressure there, for it comes as an emergency and lets everybody know that the organization is not functioning smoothly.[17]

That these mechanisms are recognized by most people was shown nicely in the series of silent films made by Hutte and Cohen. Each of ten one-minute silent films features the same two actors and the same sort of action. One man is seated at an office desk sorting through a card index. He interrupts his activity to telephone. The film then cuts to the other man who stops, knocks at the office door, enters, and approaches the man at the desk. The two then discuss some matter related to papers that the second man has with him. The two actors switched roles in random fashion throughout the ten films. Audiences were very consistent in rating the relative status of the two men. The caller was most subordinate when he stopped just inside the door and conversed with the seated man at that distance, somewhat less subordinate when he walked halfway into the room and conversed, and he was least subordinate when he walked directly across to the desk. Two other factors, the time between knocking and entry, and the time between the knock and the rising of the original occupant of the room were also related to dominance and territoriality. Status of the seated person increased with the length of time he took to respond to the knock on the door.[18]

---

[17] William F. Whyte, "The Social Structure of the Restaurant," *American Journal of Sociology*, LIV (1949), 302–8.

[18] Study cited in Tom Burns, "Nonverbal Communication," *Discovery* (October 1964), pp. 31–35.

LEADERSHIP

It is frequently necessary to distinguish between *dominance*—one individual intimidating or threatening another—and *leadership*—one individual directing the group. Among red deer the dominance shown by males during the breeding season is vastly different from the leadership by the older females who are out ahead of the group and determine its direction without the use of force. Describing a study of goats that showed that being dominant did not help an animal become a leader and vice versa, Scott hypothesized that leadership and dominance behavior are learned separately.[19] Occasionally they may conflict since one depends upon punishment and the other on reward. However, for the most part, leadership and dominance are closely related. Ethologist Ewan Grant observed all aggressive and flight reactions among a group of female mental patients and was able to discern a relatively straightforward dominance hierarchy. He also noticed that this was associated with the patient's mental condition—patients who were more in touch with reality tended to be higher along the scale. Due to this connection, and also to the greater visibility of the dominant patients, nurses were more likely to ask the dominant patients to lead the group in activities—take them out for walks or to the lunchroom. This attention from the staff reinforced the dominant patient's leadership role since she could issue directives to the other patients with the power of the staff behind her.[20]

Working with discussion groups in a cafeteria setting, Sommer showed that leaders tended to select the head position at a rectangular table and other people would arrange themselves so that they could see the leader. Visual contact with the leader seemed more important to the other people at the table than physical proximity.[21] A similar finding was obtained by Strodtbeck and Hook who recorded the seating arrangements in experimental jury sessions carried out in Chicago which were not, however, actual court cases. The experimental jurors were accompanied by a bailiff into a jury room that contained a rectangular table with one chair at the head and the foot, and five chairs on either side (1–5–1–5). The jurors' first task was to elect a

[19] Scott, *op. cit.*

[20] Ewan C. Grant, "An Ethological Description of Some Schizophrenic Patterns of Behaviour," *Proceedings of the Leeds Symposium on Behavioural Disorders*, March 25–27, 1965, Chapter 12, pp. 3–14.

[21] Robert Sommer, "Leadership and Group Geography," *Sociometry*, XXIV (1961), 99–110.

foreman, and there was a striking trend for the person seated at one of the head positions to be elected foreman. This was attributed to the "intrinsic propriety" of the chairman being at the head of the table as well as the likelihood that electing someone else would be taken as a personal rejection of the individual at the head position. It was also found that the initial choice of seats was not random. People from a higher economic class—proprietors and managers—selected head chairs more than would have been expected by chance. In electing a foreman it appeared that the jurors looked at both occupants of the head chairs and selected the one with higher status. In view of the head chair's association with leadership as well as the fact that people of higher status occupied the head chair, it was not surprising that people in the head chair participated in the discussion more than people at the other positions. Subsequent ratings by all jury members showed that the people at the head chair were considered to have made the most significant contributions to the deliberations.[22]

Leavitt was interested in communication within various shaped networks—a network was the arrangement of individuals according to the experimenter's plan. Some networks consisted of circles where messages went around the periphery, wheels where all the messages had to come into a center hub, as well as Y-shaped and incomplete circle arrangements. After the sessions the experimenter asked each group whether one member had been a leader. About half the group in circular arrangements named someone as a leader, and he was found among all positions in the circle, but 92 per cent of the groups with the wheel arrangements named leaders, and this was invariably the person at the hub.[23]

Russo asked college students to rate diagrammed seating arrangements along dimensions of friendliness, talkativeness, intimacy, and equality. The ratings along the first three dimensions correlated perfectly, with increasing physical distance indicating less acquaintance, friendliness, talkativeness, except where increased eye contact countered the effects of increased distance. The cultural influence of the head position was evident on the equality dimension—if one member of a pair were at the head position, the pair was rated as more unequal than if both people were at the sides of the table or both at the end.[24] Machotka studied the same phenomena more intensively using line drawings from well-known paintings in which various as-

[22] Fred L. Strodtbeck and L. H. Hook, "The Social Dimensions of a Twelve Man Jury Table," *Sociometry,* XXIV (1961), 397–415.

[23] Harold J. Leavitt, "Some Effects of Certain Communications Patterns on Group Performance," *Journal of Abnormal and Social Psychology,* XLVI (1951), 38–50.

[24] Nancy Russo, "Connotation of Seating Arrangements," *Cornell Journal of Social Relations,* II (1967), 37–44.

pects of body orientation, gaze, and interpersonal contact were systematically varied. Figures that were placed higher on a page but looked straight ahead, thus avoiding eye contact, were considered to be hostile, haughty, and distant, whereas other higher figures who looked directly at their partners were perceived as trying to initiate action. Another series of drawings varied arm position. A figure with his hands clasped behind his back was considered subordinate, humble, inexpressive, insignificant, and least likely to initiate action—lacking the "taut ascendance" Machotka associated with the qualities of leadership. It was the figure with his arm out as if directing the others in a firm aggressive manner who was regarded as dominant, action-initiated, expressive, and important. Another figure in the group with hands at his hips was considered self-concerned and haughty.[25] It appears that leadership can be differentiated from haughtiness in terms of this desire to communicate with other people. Leadership requires contact with others, but haughtiness requires distance. Superior height can indicate dominance, although all this must be qualified by the eye contact or head orientation of the individuals. In Charlie Chaplin's movie *The Great Dictator*, both Hitler and Mussolini attempt to stand above the other; but in paintings of the Nativity the shepherds and wise men counteract their superior height by lowering themselves or parts of their body as much as possible.

Studies of the ways in which a person's location influences his status have been infrequent, probably because experimentation requires conditions that are uncommon in nature. Typically, status and location are confounded in that prestigious individuals and leaders occupy the best places. In most organizations, office size and location are determined by rank. Space assignment policies not only indicate the role that people are expected to play but also make it difficult for people in other locations to exercise leadership. Certain exceptions to these assignment policies can be found in artificial communities or total institutions where space usage is decided on an arbitrary basis. Although spatial segregation prevails in many isolated service communities and military bases, it is still possible to find instances where several status levels share space. In housing projects for married noncommissioned officers at several British Army stations, a difference of more than one step in rank decreased contact between neighbors. This trend was sufficiently marked to warrant a recommendation against mixing ranks since this practice appeared to discourage friendships from springing up between close neighbors.[26]

[25] Pavel Machotka, "Body Movement as Communication," in *Dialogues: Vol. 2.* (Boulder, Colorado: Western Interstate Commission for Higher Education, 1965).

[26] John Madge and Janet Madge, *Survey of New Army Married Quarters* (London: Ministry of Public Buildings and Works, 1965).

There are signs that the previously accepted dominance order is weakening. There are still rich and poor people and industrialized and underdeveloped nations, but the legitimacy of the system is under serious question for the first time. There are few plausible and morally defensible explanations why one person, family, or nation should live in luxury while others live in poverty from one generation to the next. As a guide to the future, we can draw some analogy from experimental work where the deterioration of dominance relationships within a social system leads to greater reliance on territorial rights. A society compensates for blurred social distinctions by clear spatial ones—physical barriers, keep-out signs, and property restrictions. Although there are signs that some of these developments are occurring, a rigid spatial order is not likely to endure in the face of rising population density. Research with animal societies in enclosures indicates that spatial as well as social orders crumble under the onslaught of crowding. The result is extreme social disorganization of the type described in rats and mice by Calhoun. Family structure disintegrated, mothers did not care for their young, sexual perversion and cannibalism were frequent. Finally, the animals that survived became less aggressive and withdrew from social contact, cocooning as it were.[27] An American biologist visiting a laboratory in England was asked in his welcoming note by his English host to "forgive us our seemingly cold indifference. This is a small and crowded island. We can exist only by ignoring each other."

De Jonge concludes that a person can live amidst a great multitude only by showing relative indifference toward the majority of them. Only by restricting personal contact to a limited number of people is a normal life possible. De Jonge hypothesizes a complementary relationship between family and societal organization. In urban areas where population density is high, the family and home will be closed to the outsider but the larger society will be open. On the other hand, in sparsely populated rural areas the number of people that one meets is limited and the inclination to greet them and know them is greater. Society tends to be closed, but the family remains relatively open.[28] One is reminded here of the housewives who had moved from the city to the suburbs and were astonished at the way their suburban neighbors entered houses to gossip and borrow sugar without knocking.[29] An exception to this pattern occurs in urban slums where the families are relatively open but they are isolated (closed off) from the larger society.

[27] John B. Calhoun, "Population Density and Social Pathology," *Scientific American*, CCVI (1962), 139–48.

[28] Derk de Jonge, "Some Notes on Sociological Research in the Field of Housing," University of Delft, mimeo., 1967.

[29] William H. Whyte, *The Organization Man* (New York: Simon and Schuster, Inc., 1956).

Territoriality, dominance relationships, and excessive emotions are not needed when people react to one another as nonpersons. There is every indication that strong emotion is presently dysfunctional in American society. Anyone who gets too excited about anything is likely to be a danger to his neighbors and/or the government. Evolutionary biologists maintain that a behavior pattern that is dysfunctional over a long period of time is likely to be selected out. Poets, playwrights, and artists have shown prescience in describing the world of lonely, alienated individuals. However, the protagonists of Kafka, Sartre, and Ellison have typically been viewed as unusual specimens—people who thought or saw too much and were in need of therapy or religion. That this should become the typical state of affairs in society—or to put it more accurately "asociety"—is a disconcerting thought.

More use is being made of territorial mechanisms to keep density down in public areas in the face of increasing population pressures. One current example exists in state campgrounds where population pressures are severe during summer months and holidays. Some years ago most state parks were open to as many campers as could squeeze into the campgrounds. As with New York subways during rush hour, there was always room for one more. The resulting crowding not only annoyed many campers, but it also posed a threat to the parks themselves where a delicate balance between natural elements such as trees, grass, flowers, and visitors existed. A surplus of people would drive away some animals, domesticate others, attract scavengers, pollute the streams, and ruin the meadows and flowers. Crowded campgrounds also presented health, safety, crime, and refuse disposal problems.

One solution has been to divide the campgrounds up into a finite number of territories based on expert opinion as to optimal population density for the specific park. This system has kept campground occupancy to a desired level, but it has produced many complaints about the unpredictability of the system. People do not know whether they can obtain a camping spot until it is too late to go elsewhere. This has resulted in a further solidification of territoriality with the introduction in California of a computerized reservation system for camping places. A family writes several months in advance to reserve camping space in a particular park. When the system is fully operational, it will eliminate the mad scramble for campsites that begins at two o'clock in the afternoon. There will be less waste motion at the campgrounds and fewer possibilities of disputes over spots and how long a family can stay since these will be programmed beforehand. The system should work well when the number of applicants coincides with the number of available places, but during summer months and holidays, it will certainly require procedures for selecting a certain few. This brings forth dominance considerations that tend in the long run to become class oriented. Those families who can plan their vacations six months in advance, obtain and fill out the necessary application forms, and return them with the reservation fee and down payment will secure the best places. In a free market situation, the division of space becomes strongly intertwined with the existing dominance order. Space allocation not only indicates status but also reinforces it.

In summary, this chapter has outlined the close connection between space and status. Higher-ups have more and better space, as well as greater freedom to move about. This becomes institutionalized in the design and layout of buildings. An alternative form of social organization is territoriality under which individuals know where they belong spatially rather than socially. It is necessary that designers and space managers recognize the functions of these mechanisms for controlling the distribution and density of people. The next two chapters will discuss the ways in which people defend their space against invasion by others and how they maintain privacy in a crowded world. The serious tensions in both the territorial and the dominance orders in society make these pressing issues.

3

Spatial Invasion

Dear Abby: I have a pet peeve that sounds so petty and stupid that I'm almost ashamed to mention it. It is people who come and sit down beside me on the piano bench while I'm playing. I don't know why this bothers me so much, but it does. Now you know, Abby, you can't tell someone to get up and go sit somewhere else without hurting their feelings. But it would be a big relief to me if I could get them to move in a nice inoffensive way . . .

Lost Chord

Dear Lost: People want to sit beside you while you're playing because they are fascinated. Change your attitude and regard their presence as a compliment, and it might be easier to bear. P.S. You might also change your piano bench for a piano stool. (Abigail Van Buren, *San Francisco Chronicle,* May 25, 1965)

The best way to learn the location of invisible boundaries is to keep walking until somebody complains. Personal space refers to an area with invisible boundaries surrounding a person's body into which intruders may not come. Like the porcupines in Schopenhauer's fable, people like to be close enough to obtain warmth and comradeship but far enough away to avoid pricking one another. Personal space is not necessarily spherical in shape, nor does it extend equally in all directions. (People are able to tolerate closer presence of a stranger at their sides than directly in front.) It has been likened to a snail shell, a soap bubble, an aura, and "breathing room." There are major differences between cultures in the distances that people maintain—Englishmen keep further apart than Frenchmen or South Americans. Reports from Hong Kong where three million people are crowded into 12 square miles indicate that the population has adapted to the crowding reasonably well. The Hong Kong Housing Authority, now in its tenth year of operation, builds and manages low-cost apartments for families that provide approximately 35 square feet per person for living-sleeping accommodations. When the construction supervisor of one Hong Kong project was asked what the effects of doubling the amount of floor area would be upon the living patterns, he replied, "With 60 square feet per person, the tenants would sublet!" [1]

Although some people claim to see a characteristic aura around human bodies and are able to describe its color, luminosity, and dimensions, most observers cannot confirm these reports and must evolve a concept of personal space from interpersonal transactions. There is a considerable similarity between personal space and *individual distance,* or the characteristic spacing of species members. Individual distance exists only when two or more members of the same species are present and is greatly affected by population density and territorial behavior. Individual distance and personal space interact to affect the distribution of persons. The violation of individual distance is the violation of society's expectations; the invasion of personal space is an intrusion into a person's self-boundaries. Individual distance may be outside the area of personal space—conversation between two chairs across the room exceeds the boundaries of personal space, or individual distance may be less than the boundaries of personal space— sitting next to someone on a piano bench is within the expected distance but also within the bounds of personal space and may cause discomfort to the player. If there is only one individual present, there is infinite individual distance, which is why it is useful to maintain a concept of personal space, which has also been described as a *portable territory,* since the individual carries it with him wherever he goes although it disappears under certain conditions, such as crowding.

There is a formula of obscure origin that a man in a crowd requires at least two square feet. This is an absolute minimum and applies, according to one authority, to a thin man in a subway. A fat man would require twice as much space or more. Journalist Herbert Jacobs became interested in spatial behavior when he was a reporter covering political rallies. Jacobs found that estimates of crowd size varied with the observer's politics. Some estimates by police and politicians were shown to be twenty times larger than the crowd size derived from head count or aerial photographs. Jacobs found a fertile field for his research on the Berkeley campus where outdoor rallies are frequent throughout the year. He concluded that people in dense crowds have

[1] American Institute of Planners Newsletter, January 1967, p. 2.

six to eight square feet each, while in loose crowds, with people moving in and out, there is an average of ten square feet per person, Jacobs' formula is that crowd size equals length × width of the crowd divided by the appropriate correction factor depending upon whether the crowd is dense or loose. On the Berkeley campus this produced estimates reasonably close to those obtained from aerial photographs.[2]

Hospital patients complain not only that their personal space and their very bodies are continually violated by nurses, interns, and physicians who do not bother to introduce themselves or explain their activities, but that their territories are violated by well-meaning visitors who will ignore "No Visitors" signs. Frequently patients are too sick or too sensitive to repel intruders. Once surgery is finished or the medical treatment has been instituted, the patient is left to his own devices to find peace and privacy. John Lear, the science editor of the *Saturday Review,* noticed an interesting hospital game he called, "Never Close the Door," when he was a surgery patient. Although his physician wanted him protected against outside noises and distractions, the door opened at intervals, people peered in, sometimes entered, but no one ever closed the door. When Lear protested, he was met by hostile looks and indignant remarks such as, "I'm only trying to do my job, Mister." It was never clear to Lear why the job—whatever it was—required the intruder to leave the door ajar afterwards.[3]

Spatial invasions are not uncommon during police interrogations. One police textbook recommends that the interrogator should sit close to the suspect, with no table or desk between them, since "an obstruction of any sort affords the subject a certain degree of relief and confidence not otherwise obtainable." [4] At the beginning of the session, the officer's chair may be two or three feet away, "but after the interrogation is under way the interrogator should move his chair in closer so that ultimately one of the subject's knees is just about in between the interrogator's two knees." [5]

Lovers pressed together close their eyes when they kiss. On intimate occasions the lights are typically dim to reduce not only the distracting external cues but also to permit two people to remain close together. Personal space is a culturally acquired daylight phenomenon. Strangers are affected differently than friends by a loss of personal space. During rush hour, subway riders lower their eyes and sometimes "freeze" or

[2] H. Jacobs, "How Big Was the Crowd?" Talk given at California Journalism Conference, Sacramento, February 24–25, 1967.

[3] John Lear, "What's Wrong with American Hospitals?" *Saturday Review* (February 4, 1967), pp. 59–60.

[4] F. E. Inbau and J. E. Reid, *Criminal Interrogation and Confessions* (Toronto: Burns and MacEachern, 1963).

[5] Inbau and Reid, *op. cit.*

become rigid as a form of minimizing unwanted social intercourse. Boy-meets-girl on a crowded rush hour train would be a logical plot for an American theater based largely in New York City, but it is rarely used. The idea of meeting someone under conditions where privacy, dignity, and individuality are so reduced is difficult to accept. A driver can make another exceedingly nervous by tailgating. Highway authorities recommend a "space cushion" of at least one car length for every ten miles per hour of speed. You can buy a bumper sticker or a lapel button with the message "If you can read this, you're too close." A perceptive suburban theater owner noticed the way crowds arranged themselves in his lobby for different pictures. His lobby was designed to hold approximately 200 customers who would wait behind a roped area for the theater to clear.

> When we play a [family picture like] *Mary Poppins, Born Free,* or *The Cardinal,* we can line up only about 100 to 125 people. These patrons stand about a foot apart and don't touch the person next to them. But when we play a [sex comedy like] *Tom Jones* or *Irma la Douce,* we can get 300 to 350 in the same space. These people stand so close to each other you'd think they were all going to the same home at the end of the show! [6]

Animal studies indicate that individual distance is learned during the early years. At some stage early in his life the individual learns how far he must stay from species members. When he is deprived of contact with his own kind, as in isolation studies, he cannot learn proper spacing, which sets him up as a failure in subsequent social intercourse—he comes too close and evokes threat displays or stays too far away to be considered a member of the group. Newborn of many species can be induced to follow novel stimuli in place of their parents. If a newly hatched chicken is separated from his mother and shown a flashing light instead, on subsequent occasions he will follow the flashing light rather than his mother. The distance he remains behind the object is a function of its size; young chicks will remain further behind a large object than a small one.[7]

Probably the most feasible method for exploring individual distance and personal space with their invisible boundaries is to approach people and observe their reactions. Individual distance is not an absolute figure but varies with the relationship between the individuals, the distance at which others in the situation are placed, and the bodily

[6] Bob Ellison, "If the Movie Is Comic, Sex Is OK, in Suburbia," *Chicago Sun Times,* Jan. 15, 1967, Section 3, p. 4.

[7] Peter H. Klopfer and J. P. Hailman, *An Introduction to Animal Behavior* (Englewood Cliffs, N.J.: Prentice-Hall, Inc., 1967).

orientations of the individuals one to another. The most systematic work along these lines has been undertaken by the anthropologist Ray Birdwhistell who records a person's response with zoom lenses and is able to detect even minute eye movements and hand tremors as the invader approaches the emotionally egotistic zone around the victim.[8]

One of the earliest attempts to invade personal space on a systematic basis was undertaken by Williams, who wanted to learn how different people would react to excessive closeness. Classifying students as introverts or extroverts on the basis of their scores on a personality test, he placed each individual in an experimental room and then walked toward the person, telling him to speak out as soon as he (Williams) came too close. Afterward he used the reverse condition, starting at a point very close and moving away until the person reported that he was too far away for comfortable conversation. His results showed that introverts kept people at a greater conversational distance than extroverts.[9]

The same conclusion was reached by Leipold, who studied the distance at which introverted and extroverted college students placed themselves in relation to an interviewer in either a stress or a nonstress situation. When the student entered the experimental room, he was given either the stress, praise, or neutral instructions. The stress instructions were, "We feel that your course grade is quite poor and that you have not tried your best. Please take a seat in the next room and Mr. Leipold will be in shortly to discuss this with you." The neutral control instructions read, "Mr. Leipold is interested in your feelings about the introductory course. Would you please take a seat in the next room." After the student had entered and seated himself, Mr. Leipold came in, recorded the student's seating position, and conducted the interview. The results showed that students given praise sat closest to Leipold's chair, followed by those in the neutral condition, with students given the stress instructions maintaining the most distance from Leipold's chair behind the desk. It was also found that introverted and anxious individuals sat further away from him than did extroverted students with a lower anxiety level.[10]

Glen McBride has done some excellent work on the spatial behaviors of fowl, not only in captivity but in their feral state on islands off the Australian coast. He has recently turned his attention to human spatial behavior using the galvanic skin response (GSR) as an index

[8] R. L. Birdwhistell, *Introduction to Kinesics* (Washington: Foreign Service Institute, 1952).

[9] John L. Williams, "Personal Space and its Relation to Extroversion-Introversion" (Master's thesis, University of Alberta, 1963).

[10] William E. Leipold, "Psychological Distance in a Dyadic Interview" (Ph.D. thesis, University of North Dakota, 1963).

of emotionality. The GSR picks up changes in skin conductivity that relate to stress and emotional behavior. The same principle underlies what is popularly known as the lie detector test. McBride placed college students in a chair from which they were approached by both male and female experimenters as well as by paper figures and nonhuman objects. It was found that GSR was greatest (skin resistance was least) when a person was approached frontally, whereas a side approach yielded a greater response than a rear approach. The students reacted more strongly to the approach of someone of the opposite sex than to someone of the same sex. Being touched by an object produced less of a GSR than being touched by a person.[11]

A similar procedure without the GSR apparatus was used by Argyle and Dean, who invited their subjects to participate in a perceptual experiment in which they were to "stand as close as comfortable to see well" to a book, a plaster head, and a cut-out life-size photograph of the senior author with his eyes closed and another photograph with his eyes open. Among other results, it was found that the subjects placed themselves closer to the eyes-closed photograph than the eyes-open photograph.[12] Horowitz, Duff, and Stratton used a similar procedure with schizophrenic and nonschizophrenic mental patients. Each individual was instructed to walk over to a person, or in another condition a hatrack, and the distance between the goal and his stopping place was measured. It was found that most people came closer to the hatrack than they did to another person. Each tended to have a characteristic individual distance that was relatively stable from one situation to another, but was shorter for inanimate objects than for people. Schizophrenics generally kept greater distance between themselves and others than did nonpatients.[13] The last finding is based on average distance values, which could be somewhat inflated by a few schizophrenics who maintain a large individual distance. Another study showed that some schizophrenic patients sat "too close" and made other people nervous by doing this. However, it was more often the case that schizophrenics maintained excessive physical distance to reduce the prospects of unwanted social intercourse.[14]

In order to explore personal space using the invasion technique, but to avoid the usual connotations surrounding forced close proximity to strangers, my own method was to undertake the invasion in a place

[11] Glen McBride, M. G. King, and J. W. James, "Social Proximity Effects on GSR in Adult Humans," *Journal of Psychology*, LXI (1965), 153–57.

[12] Michael Argyle and Janet Dean, "Eye Contact, Distance, and Affiliation," *Sociometry*, XXVIII (1965), 289–304.

[13] Mardi J. Horowitz, D. F. Duff, and L. O. Stratton, "Body-Buffer Zone," *Archives of General Psychiatry*, XI (1964), 651–56.

[14] Robert Sommer, "Studies in Personal Space," *Sociometry*, XXII (1959), 247–60.

where the usual sanctions of the outside world did not apply. Deliberate invasions of personal space seem more feasible and appropriate inside a mental hospital than outside. Afterward, it became apparent that this method could be adapted for use in other settings such as the library in which Nancy Russo spent many hours sitting too close to other girls.

The first study took place at a 1500-bed mental institution situated in parklike surroundings in northern California. Most wards were unlocked, and patients spent considerable time out of doors. In wooded areas it was common to see patients seated under the trees, one to a bench or knoll. The wards within the buildings were relatively empty during the day because of the number of patients outside as well as those who worked in hospital industry. This made it possible for patients to isolate themselves from others by finding a deserted area on the grounds or remaining in an almost empty building. At the outset I spent considerable time observing how patients isolated themselves from one another. One man typically sat at the base of a fire escape so he was protected by the bushes on one side and the railing on the other. Others would lie on benches in remote areas and feign sleep if approached. On the wards a patient might sit in a corner and place magazines or his coat on adjacent seats to protect the space. The use of belongings to indicate possession is very common in bus stations, cafeterias, waiting rooms, but the mental patient is limited in using this method since he lacks possessions. Were he to own a magazine or book, which is unlikely, and left it on an empty chair, it would quickly vanish.

Prospective victims had to meet three criteria—male, sitting alone, and not engaged in any definite activity such as reading or playing cards. When a patient fitting these criteria was located, I walked over and sat beside him without saying a word. If the patient moved his chair or slid further down the bench, I moved a like distance to keep the space between us to about six inches. In all sessions I jiggled my key ring a few times to assert my dominance, the key being a mark of status in a mental hospital. It can be noted that these sessions not only invaded the patient's personal space but also the nurse's territory. It bothered the nurses to see a high status person (jacket, white shirt, tie, and the title "Doctor") entering their wards and sitting among the patients. The dayroom was the patients' territory vis-à-vis the nurses, but it was the nurses' territory vis-à-vis the medical staff. Control subjects were selected from other patients who were seated some distance away but whose actions could be observed.

Within two minutes, all of the control subjects remained but one-third of the invasion victims had been driven away. Within nine minutes, fully half of the victims had departed compared with only 8 per cent of the controls (see Fig. 1). Flight was a gross reaction to the intrusion; there were many more subtle indications of the patient's

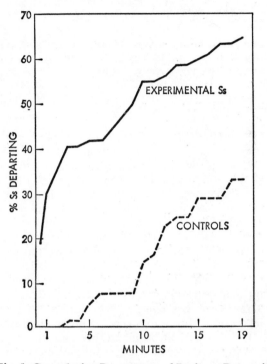

Fig. 1. Cumulative Percentage of Patients Departing at Each One-Minute Interval.

discomfort. The typical sequence was for the victim to face away immediately, pull in his shoulders, and place his elbows at his sides. Facing away was an almost universal reaction among the victims, often coupled with hands placed against the chin as a buffer. Records obtained during the notetaking sessions illustrate this defensive pattern.

Example A
    10:00. Seat myself next to a patient, about sixty years of age; he is smoking and possibly watching TV.
    10:04. Patient rubs his face briefly with the back of his hand.
    10:05. Patient breathes heavily, still smoking, and puts his ashes into a tin can. He looks at his watch occasionally.

10:06. He puts out his cigarette, rubs his face with the back of his hand. Still watching TV.

10:12. Patient glances at his watch, flexes his fingers.

10:13. Patient rises, walks over and sits at a seat several chairs over. Observation ended.

Example B

8:46. Seat myself next to a 60-year-old man who looks up as I enter the room. As I sit down, he begins talking to himself, snuffs out his cigarette, rises, and walks across the room. He asks a patient on the other side of the room, "You want me to sit here?" He starts arranging the chairs against the opposite wall and finally sits down.

Ethologist Ewan Grant has made a detailed analysis of the patient's micro behaviors drawing much inspiration from the work of Tinbergen[15] as well as his own previous studies with colonies of monkeys and rats. Among a group of confined mental patients he determined a relatively straightforward dominance hierarchy based on aggression-flight encounters between individuals. Aggressive acts included threat gestures ("a direct look plus a sharp movement of the head towards the other person"), frowns, and hand-raising. Flight behaviors included retreat, bodily evasions, closed eyes, withdrawing the chin into the chest, hunching, and crouching. These defensive behaviors occurred when a dominant individual sat too close to a subordinate. This could be preceded by some overt sign of tension such as rocking, leg swinging, or tapping. Grant describes one such encounter: "A lower ranking member of the group is sitting in a chair; a dominant approaches and sits near her. The first patient begins to rock and then frequently, on one of the forward movements, she gets up and moves away." [16]

In seventeen British old folks homes Lipman found that most of the patients had favorite chairs that they considered "theirs." Their title to these chairs was supported by the behavior of both patients and staff. A newly admitted inmate had great difficulty in finding a chair that was not owned by anyone. Typically he occupied one seat and then another until he found one that was "unowned." When he sat in someone else's chair, he was told to move away in no uncertain terms.[17] Accidental invasions were an accepted fact of life in these old folks homes. It is possible to view them as a hazing or initiation ceremony for new residents to teach them the informal institutional rules and

[15] N. Tinbergen, *Social Behaviour in Animals* (London: Methuen & Co. Ltd., 1953).

[16] Grant, *op. cit.*

[17] Alan Lipman, "Building Design and Social Interaction," *The Architects Journal,* CXLVII (1968), 23–30.

understandings. Such situations illustrate the importance of knowing not only how people mark out and personalize spaces, but how they respond to intrusions.

We come now to the sessions Nancy Russo conducted in the study hall of a college library, a large high-ceilinged room with book-lined walls. Because this is a study area, students typically try to space themselves as far as possible from one another. Systematic observations over a two-year period disclosed that the first occupants of the room generally sat one to a table at end chairs. Her victims were all females sitting alone with at least one book in front of them and empty chairs on either side and across. In other words, the prospective victim was sitting in an area surrounded by empty chairs, which indicated something about her preference for solitude as well as making an invasion relatively easy. The second female to meet these criteria in each session and who was visible to Mrs. Russo served as a control. Each control subject was observed from a distance and no invasion was attempted. There were five different approaches used in the invasions—sometimes Mrs. Russo would sit alongside the subject, other times directly across from her, and so forth. All of these were violations of the typical seating norms in the library, which required a newcomer to sit at a considerable distance from those already seated unless the room was crowded.

Occupying the adjacent chair and moving it closer to the victim, produced the quickest departures, and there was a slight but also significant difference between the other invasion locations and the control condition. There were wide individual differences in the ways the victims reacted—there is no single reaction to someone's sitting too close; there are defensive gestures, shifts in posture, and attempts to move away. If these fail or are ignored by the invader, or he shifts position too, the victim eventually takes to flight. Crook measured spacing of birds in three ways: *arrival distance* or how far from settled birds a newcomer will land, *settled distance* or the resultant distance after adjustments have occurred, and the *distance after departure* or how far apart birds remain after intermediate birds have left.[18] The methods employed in the mental hospital and portions of the library study when the invader shifted his position if the victim moved, maintained the *arrival distance* and did not permit the victim to achieve a comfortable *settled distance*. It is noteworthy that the preponderance of flight reactions occurred under these conditions. There was a dearth of direct verbal responses to the invasions. Only two of the 69 mental

[18] J. H. Crook, "The Basis of Flock Organization in Birds," in *Current Problems in Animal Behavior*, eds. W. H. Thorpe and O. L. Zangwill (London: Cambridge University Press, 1961).

patients and one of the 80 students asked the invader to move over. This provides support for Edward Hall's view that "we treat space somewhat as we treat sex. It is there, but we don't talk about it." [19]

Architecture students on the Berkeley campus now undertake behavioral studies as part of their training. One team noted the reactions of students on outdoor benches when an experimenter joined them on the same bench. The occupant shifted position more frequently in a specified time-frame and left the bench earlier than control subjects who were alone. A second team was interested in individual distance on ten-foot benches. When the experimenter seated himself one foot from the end of the bench, three-quarters of the next occupants sat six to eight feet away, and almost half placed books or coats as barriers between themselves and the experimenter. Another two students studied eyeblink and shifts in body position as related to whether a stranger sat facing someone or sat facing away. Observations were made by a second experimenter using binoculars from a distance. A male stranger directly facing a female markedly increased her eyeblink rate as well as body movements but had no discernible effect on male subjects.[20]

The different ways in which victims react to invasions may also be due to variations in the perception of the expected distance or in the ability to concentrate. It has been demonstrated that the individual distance between birds is reduced when one bird's attention is riveted to some activity.[21] The invasions can also be looked at as nonverbal communication with the victims receiving messages ranging from "This girl considers me a nonperson" to "This girl is making a sexual advance." The fact that regressed and "burnt out" patients can be moved from their places by sheer propinquity is of theoretical and practical importance. In view of the difficulty that nurses and others have in obtaining any response at all from these patients, it is noteworthy that an emotion sufficient to generate flight can be produced simply by sitting alongside them. More recently we have been experimenting with visual invasions, or attempts to dislodge someone from his place by staring directly at him. In the library at least, the evil eye seems less effective than a spatial invasion since the victims are able to lose themselves in their books. If they could not escape eye contact so easily, this method might be more effective. Mrs. Russo

[19] Edward T. Hall, *The Silent Language* (Garden City, New York: Doubleday & Company, Inc., 1959).

[20] These were term projects in Architecture 140 taught by Professor Richard Seaton. They are available on microfilm from the Dept. of Architecture, University of California, Berkeley 94704.

[21] Crook, *op. cit.*

was sensitive to her own feelings during these sessions and described how she "lost her cool" when a victim looked directly toward her. Eye contact produced a sudden realization that "this is a human being," which subsided when the victim turned away. Civil rights demonstrators attempt to preserve their human dignity by maintaining eye contact with their adversaries.

There are other sorts of invasions—auditory assaults in which strangers press personal narratives on hapless seatmates on airplanes and buses, and olfactory invasions long celebrated in television commercials. Another interesting situation is the two-person invasion. On the basis of animal work, particularly on chickens crowded in coops, it was discovered that when a subordinate encounters a dominant at very close quarters where flight is difficult or impossible, the subordinate is likely to freeze in his tracks until the dominant departs or at least looks away. Two faculty members sitting on either side of a student or two physicians on either side of a patient's bed would probably produce this type of freezing. The victim would be unlikely to move until he had some sign that the dominants had their attention elsewhere.

The library studies made clear that an important consideration in defining a spatial invasion is whether the parties involved perceive one another as persons. A nonperson cannot invade someone's personal space any more than a tree or chair can. It is common under certain conditions for one person to react to another as an object or part of the background. Examples would be the hospital nurses who discuss a patient's condition at his bedside, seemingly oblivious to his presence, the Negro maid in the white home who serves dinner while the husband and wife discuss the race question, and the janitor who enters an office without knocking to empty the wastebaskets while the occupant is making an important phone call. Many subway riders who have adjusted to crowding through psychological withdrawal prefer to treat other riders as nonpersons and keenly resent situations, such as a stop so abrupt that the person alongside pushes into them *and then apologizes,* when the other rider becomes a person. There are also riders who dislike the lonely alienated condition of subway travel and look forward to emergency situations in which people become real. When a lost child is looking for his mother, a person has been hurt, or a car is stalled down the tracks, strangers are allowed to talk to one another.

It is paradoxical but perhaps not illogical that the best way to study invasions of privacy is to stage them deliberately. The results of this research will be more evident in the next chapter, which examines the defensive measures that people take to protect themselves against invasions, and also in the last half of the book, which describes certain building types such as hospitals and libraries where privacy is of paramount consideration.

4

In Defense of Privacy

"This place is ours," said one of the motorcycle gang. "This and the Aloha. This is our territory. You're a surfer, you come in here and you're dead."

There has been a great deal of discussion recently both in the courts and among civil liberties groups about the individual's right to privacy. According to present interpretations, the right to be let alone is not provided in the Constitution nor in common law. However, many states have passed laws that permit an individual whose picture or name is used in an advertisement without his permission to collect damages. This doctrine has been extended to cover people's private lives and acts that are not in themselves newsworthy. Prohibition against unreasonable search and seizure as well as fifth-amendment protection against mandatory self-incrimination also operate to preserve the individual's right to be let alone. Thus far the court cases have been mainly concerned with visual and auditory privacy—protection against bugging devices, music on public buses, and police interrogation without counsel present. Protection against physical intrusion of other people is provided by laws relating to private property and trespass. The latter do not apply in the public spaces where people spend more and more of their lives. A patron in a public library or restaurant has no legal right to privacy, although someone who annoys him may be charged with disorderly conduct or disturbing the peace. It is unlikely that these charges could be pressed if one person simply walked in and sat down next to another, even though this violated local mores and invaded personal space. The individual whose personal space is invaded this way is obliged to get up and sit elsewhere. There is a gray area in cases of tailgating on the highways and physical intrusion in restaurants—cases now in the domain of manners and customs but which occasionally spill over into the courts.

Even clear territorial boundaries based on legal title do not in themselves guarantee privacy or security. Not only must illegal entry by thieves be considered, but also the nuisance calls by salesmen and tradesmen, as well as the quasi-legal incursions by gas company employees, tax assessors, health inspectors, and policemen. A recent case before the Supreme Court raised the issue of whether a health inspector may enter a private home on a routine inspection without the benefit of a search warrant. Commenting on the case publicly, Chief Justice Warren declared that the fundamental issue was "the right to privacy." The defendant, Mr. Roland Camara, was sentenced under a section of the Housing Code that allows a six-month jail term or $500 fine for barring entry to a health inspector. A parallel case arose in Seattle involving the fire department's right to visit premises without a court warrant. On June 4, 1967, the Supreme Court, in a six to three decision, agreed with the defendants that householders had the right to refuse to admit municipal health, welfare, and safety inspectors unless they possessed valid search warrants.

Several recent court cases involving protest demonstrations have made ownership of public spaces more than an academic issue. In January 1967 three demonstrators at the Port Chicago Naval Station who had been arrested on trespassing charges were released when the Federal Government could not prove ownership of the gate outside the Navy Yard. In the same month a key issue in the trial of several Berkeley demonstrators was the ownership of the Student Union Building where the demonstrations took place. Defense attorney Melvin Belli contended that the University did not own the building and therefore the defendants were not trespassing on University property. A University Vice Chancellor conceded that he did not know who really owned the building. Another prosecution witness said that although the Associated Students owned it, the Associated Students were an arm of the University controlled by the Administration.

A homeowner in Saskatchewan, Canada, who is convicted of certain offenses, can have his house declared a public place. If he repeats the offense, not only does his home "cease to become a dwelling place," but so does every other place he visits, including hotel rooms, for the next five years.[1] The reason for this unusual "socializing of space" is that drinking can be regulated in public places by the Provincial liquor

---

[1] D. Marshall, "The Autocrats Who Issue the Drinking Man's Fiats," *MacLeans* (March 1967), p. 1.

authority, which is reluctant to reach into private homes. By declaring private homes to be public places, their work becomes easier. Another sort of public private space exists in marginal communities like New York City's East Village:

> Groups of ten people in one apartment are not unusual. Sometimes it becomes a narrow line between the host and the homeless and, in cobwebs of sublets and promised rent, an apartment may become a transient domain and the original host eventually forgotten.[2]

Crowding gives rise to the need for social regulations that limit the unwanted intimacy which would be likely to arise in the absence of physical barriers. Noting that spatial segregation is a pervasive principle of social organization, researchers indicate that it protects the superordinate against overly intimate exposure to subordinates, maintains physical barriers to socially proscribed sexual arousal and intimacy, and protects the in-group against undue external influence. Under crowded conditions, social norms for maintaining privacy partially substitute for the lack of physical devices.[3]

In civil defense shelter studies many people moved about the shelter only when they needed to go to the lavatory or when shelter routine required their movement. Initially, a number of minor accidents occurred as a result of sudden movements under crowded conditions—elbows in the ribs, bumping, spilled coffee. Gradually the shelter inhabitants slowed down their movements.[4] Cocooning, or mutual withdrawal from social intercourse, is another common reaction. The best descriptions of overcrowding do not dwell at length on the shortage of space or restricted movement in an abstract sense, but what this means in terms of interpersonal relations. The following article is entitled "What Is a Slum?"

> It is overcrowding, but few people know what this really means.
> Overcrowding means never a moment of privacy for husband and wife to build an emotional life together, never a night's sleep unbroken by crying, fretful children in a crib next to the bed, in the kitchen, in the living room, never more than 15 feet away. . . . It's nowhere to go to rest and relax. It's a television set on a broken table in the living room—the only furniture that isn't for sleeping or eating—but who can watch it, the children must get to sleep.

[2] Don McNeill, "Living Without an Address on the Lower East Side," *The Village Voice* (December 22, 1966), p. 28.

[3] A. D. Biderman, M. Louria, and J. Bacchus, *Historical Incidents of Extreme Overcrowding* (Washington: Bureau of Social Science Research, 1963).

[4] J. W. Altman, *Psychological and Social Adjustment in a Simulated Shelter* (Santa Barbara: American Institute for Research, 1960).

It's nowhere to drink a glass of beer—but out in the bar. . . . It's no place to cook three meals a day but a broken stove and a leaky sink, and no place to serve them. It's nowhere for children to do homework. . . . It's no place to pretty up to call one's own. . . . It's children sent out to the streets . . . anything for a minute's peace . . . but no way to get it.[5]

Although crowding requires voluntary or involuntary confinement, confinement is not always accompanied by crowding. Life at Antarctic stations provides situations in which relatively few people occupy many buildings in addition to vast expanses of space outside, but must still come together to work, eat, sleep, and so forth. Avoidance as a means of reducing tension is relatively ineffective under conditions of confinement. Here one finds the counterpart of the "new morality" in interpersonal relations that Altman found in simulated shelters. Men at Antarctic stations keep a tight rein on their emotions: "Quarrels serious enough to end in a brawl back home rarely terminate in physical violence in Antarctica. Men seem to be innately aware of the irrevocable nature of an actual blow in an environment where for months to come one must daily meet one's antagonist face-to-face." [6] In prisons this reaction is often described as "cooling it." One defends against the possibilities of intrusion and unwanted contact by limiting his excursions and averting his eyes when he moves about.

Area shape has a significant effect on defensive capability. Generally speaking an irregularly shaped area is difficult to protect. Furthermore its irregularity is likely to be accompanied by ambiguity and hence more frequent disputes over the ownership of particular segments. A compact circular or square area makes defense easier whereas uneven boundaries between areas are likely to increase tension. The recent treaty that smooths the boundary between the United States and Mexico in the Juarez-El Paso area illustrates this. A piece of land called Cordova "Island" had been a piece of Mexican territory on the United States side of the river because of a shift in the river channel. The unusual shape of the boundary at this area, as well as the uncertain legal status of adjacent areas created considerable tension. Transportation routes through El Paso were distorted by the presence of the disputed zone—rail lines, expressways, irrigation canals, and power lines all detoured around the "island." The "island" itself was completely unused even though there was great pressure for residential

[5] Jeanne Goodwin, "What Is a Slum?" *The Independent* (February 1964), p. 4. Reprinted by permission of Lyle Stuart, Inc.

[6] Phillip Law, "Some Psychological Aspects of Life at an Antarctic Station," *Discovery*, XXI (October 1960), 431–37.

sites on both sides of the border, and the disputed area developed into a slum since nationals of neither country were willing to risk investment in developing land of uncertain title. With the exchange of territory resulting from the treaty, which gave Mexico 264 acres while the United States received 193 acres, the border was considerably smoothed, permitting orderly development of residential sites, boundary crossings, as well as more direct transportation routes.[7]

The study of territorial boundaries and their legal import is a labyrinthine topic, but a great deal is known about ways that species other than man mark out their territories. Some birds use songs during the mating season to keep others away, a bear will claw the bark from tree trunks, a deer will secrete a smelly substance from a gland near his nostrils, and a wolf may urinate at the periphery of his territory. One can learn what benefits are bestowed by a territory by examining the area to see what it supplies in the way of food, shelter, protection from predators, and so forth. It has been found, for example, that animal territories generally become larger when food is in short supply and shrink when food is plentiful. We can ask the same sorts of questions about spaces that individuals defend—what does a student gain from selecting an end chair facing the back wall; why do the first patrons in a restaurant face outward with their backs to the wall. When we understand the functions served by a given space, we can predict how strongly it will be defended and the sorts of defensive tactics likely to be used. Even if we do not accept the idea of instinctive territoriality in humans, it is still apparent that people actively defend certain spaces against intruders using the entire repertoire of defensive techniques in the animal kingdom as well as a few new ones. Increasing population density makes it obvious that not everyone will have legal title to a land area. By building upward, it is possible to guarantee everyone an enclosure of his own as well as dominion over the enclosed space. However, a man will be spending even more of his life in space he does not own or control. We must understand how he can maintain feelings of privacy and individuality in nonowned space. Later on we shall examine the ways in which an individual personalizes his immediate environment—his office, dormitory room, or summer cabin.

Lyman and Scott distinguish four types of territories in human societies: public territories, home territories, interactional territories, and body territories. Public territories such as courtyards and parks provide the citizen with freedom of access but not necessarily of ac-

[7] John D. Nystuen, "Boundary Shapes and Boundary Problems," *Peace Research Society Papers*, VII (1967), 108–28.

tion. Home territories are public areas taken over by groups or individuals. Examples would include children's makeshift clubhouses, homosexual bars, and coffeehouses that cater to habitués. In each case the regular patrons have a sense of intimacy and control over the area. Interactional territories are areas where social gatherings may occur; they have clearly marked boundaries and rules of access and egress. Lastly there are territories encompassing the body, which we have called personal space, which are most private and inviolate spaces belonging to the individual. The authors distinguish three forms of territorial encroachment: violation (unwarranted use of the territory), invasion (the physical presence of an intruder within the boundaries of the territory), and contamination (rendering a territory impure with respect to its definition and usage).[8]

Animals are no more trusting than people about allowing strangers of the same species on their territory. Marine birds such as gulls and terns occupy cliffside ledges. Because of limited space, territories are reduced to small areas around the nest. The parents take turns foraging for food over the water, and when one returns to the nest, the host forces it to undergo a recognition ceremony before it is admitted. The biologist Guhl likens this to the ceremonies of apartment and home dwellers.[9] Strangers use the doorbell or take the consequences, but children are permitted to roam over the area and do not respect the artificial boundaries of suburbia. To children the hedgerows, ground cover, and trees are more interesting for their intrinsic properties than as territorial markers. An article in the *California Law Review* describes youngsters as "unreliable and irresponsible people, who are quite likely to do almost anything. In particular, they have a deplorable tendency to stray upon land which does not belong to them, and to meddle with what they find there." [10] Even worse than invading other people's territories, is the way in which children are likely to territorialize public areas by means of clubhouses, ball parks, and street corner societies. Subject always to official harassment by the police and other adults who claim the street is public territory, youths redefine these adults as nonpersons whose presence on the youths' "turf" does not challenge the latter's proprietorship.[11]

Recognition ceremonies deserve more attention than we can give them here. One reason why our research invasions were so effective in

---

[8] Stanford M. Lyman and Marvin B. Scott, "Territoriality: A Neglected Sociological Dimension," *Social Problems*, XV (1967), 236–49.

[9] Guhl, *op. cit.*

[10] William Plosser, "Trespassing Children," *California Law Review* (August, 1959), p. 427.

[11] Lyman and Scott, *op. cit.*

driving people from their places is that the invader refused to show the proper deferential gestures as he violated the local seating norms. The invader did not apologize or show any respect for the victim; he treated him as a nonperson lacking in humanity and territorial rights. The usual procedure at a public cafeteria where there are many empty seats is for the standing person to approach the person seated and say, "Is this seat taken?" or at least lower his eyes as he sits down. At times of high density, occupancy of the last vacant seat at a table is not considered an invasion, and a mere lowering of eyes will suffice. On a bus or plane the intruder keeps his eyes straight ahead as he sits down and only gradually finds a point of focus closer to the seatmate whose privacy he has disturbed. A doctor visiting a patient in hospital keeps on his hat and overcoat as he strides over to examine the patient. When the same doctor visits the patient's own home, he comes through the front door hat in hand, removes his overcoat, and walks about humbly.

Defense of territories hinges on visible boundaries and markers, but the defense of personal space whose boundaries are invisible is a matter of gesture, posture, and choosing a location that conveys a clear meaning to others. In many situations, defense of personal space is so entangled with defense of an immediate territory that one sees them as part of a single process—the defense of privacy—that involves fundamental questions of space usage and property rights. In both the animal kingdom and world politics, an area that cannot be defended against intruders is not considered a private territory or domain. The three-mile coastal limit was originally based on the maximum range of coastal artillery batteries with the idea that a country could not claim any more territory than it could defend. Society has established courts, police, and armies to defend and adjudicate territorial claims, but the Camara case of the health inspector and the Seattle case of the fire inspector involve the individual's protecting his property rights against intrusion by society's duly constituted representatives.

To study the ways a person protects his privacy, we worked in the library study halls used previously. Few places make as strict a demand upon the physical setting to guarantee privacy as the library reading area. It is one of the few places where interaction between people is actively discouraged. Museums, art galleries, and government buildings allow conversation, which, in the view of many librarians, would impede the concentration that readers need. There are library patrons who like to chat while they read and prefer to have refreshments close by, and new libraries often contain special rooms to satisfy the needs of gregarious readers as well as to get them out of the way of people who prefer quiet and solitude. Although silence and respect for privacy can be encouraged and maintained through official regulations, social disapproval, and staff surveillance, these tasks become much easier and sometimes unnecessary in the proper library environment.

These study halls also provide a good illustration of the way that territorial behavior regulates population density. The presence of six chairs on each side of the table guaranteed that no more than twelve individuals would occupy the table, even though there was space for several others. If a student were so inclined, he could have pulled up an additional chair. Moving chairs was a common practice in the college cafeteria both during mealtime and nonmeal hours when it was used as a study hall and lounge. If five students entered the cafeteria together, it was routine for one to pull over a chair from another table and convert the four-chair into a five-chair table. However, during two years of observations, this never occurred in the reference room. No matter how great the pressure on the study facilities, room density was limited to one person per station at the eighteen tables. This is similar in appearance, although not in mechanism, to the situation of the caterpillars described by Andrewartha who live no more than one to an apple. The maximum population of codlin could be predicted by counting the number of apples in an area. If there is already a worm in an apple, the next worm goes elsewhere and finds an apple or dies, even though there is sufficient room and food in a single apple for several worms. This protects the codlin against the possibility of crowding, overpopulation, and food shortages.[12]

Library readers protect their privacy in several ways, sometimes through offensive displays and other times through defensive measures. The former are based on the idea that the best defense is a good offense and include both threat positions and postures. Position refers to a person's location in the room—the occupant of a corner location conveys a different meaning to a newcomer than one in the center of a room. This is particularly true in bars and other public places where people are likely to meet, as well as parties and social gatherings, where some locations, reinforced by certain postures and attempts to establish eye contact, indicate a desire to meet others. Whereas position refers to a person's location with reference to external coordinates, posture describes his particular stance—whether he spreads out his belongings "as if he owned the place," or pulls himself in to take up as little room as possible. Gesture can also be used to defend a given

[12] H. G. Andrewartha, *Introduction to the Study of Animal Populations* (Chicago: University of Chicago Press, 1961), p. 131.

area, a person indicating by his expression that he is receptive for company or prefers to be by himself. Biologists speak of agonistic displays that keep other species members away through threats of aggressive attack. They serve to reduce overt physical combat by substituting rituals of approach, display, ritualized struggle, and retreat. A given area can be defended by any combination of position, posture, and gesture. Avoidance works best in a room with many corners, alcoves, and side areas hidden from view. Offensive display is most effective when a person can use features of the landscape to reinforce his dominance and control access and egress. If he can hold the high ground, he should be able to dominate the area effectively. Overtly aggressive reactions to the approach of a newcomer, such as profanity, insults, or physical assault, rarely occur in a library where norms for individual privacy are well established. A comparable investigation of space ownership in a teenage club might come up with very different findings. In dyadic encounters in which there is competition for a particular area, the incumbent's decision to retreat or to stand and fight are based on assumptions about the character of the invader. If newcomers are easily intimidated, an agonistic display can secure a choice area with minimal effort. Retreat usually requires a person to go to some remote and less desirable section whereas an offensive posture can conceivably hold the best location. However, if the intruder is aggressive and willing to risk combat and the tension that will ensue from an invasion, the exposed posture and position required by agonistic display leave the defender highly vulnerable. A London prostitute describes the disadvantages of a center location in this way:

> This is my favourite table, and here I can sit with my back against the wall, facing the door. Here is a vantage point from which entries and exits can be observed without too much effort. Nobody can get behind me, and there is safety in this.
>
> If there is any trouble, if fighting breaks out for any reason—for, though there seems to be little in the air tonight, violence breeds fast in Soho—a wall position is the best to be in. In anger or in fear, I have noticed that men seek the nearest open space for maximum freedom of movement, or chance of flight, until the point when the weaker is forced towards a corner, by which time one has usually managed to duck or wriggle out of range. In the centre of a room, however alert you are you can be knocked out of your chair by scuffling men before the first blow has landed, and if you are lucky enough to get back on your feet unharmed you will probably find yourself in the heart of the battle, in which several outsiders will by this time have involved themselves.[13]

[13] Anonymous, *Streetwalker* (New York: Dell Publishing Co., 1961), p. 40.

To sit in the middle of a long table will protect the entire table against timid invaders who will shrink away rather than risk the occupant's displeasure, yet aggressive intruders will be able to surround the occupant on all sides, something that would place him in an extremely uncomfortable position. Against an aggressive invader, a remote position in a corner or alcove will make it physically impossible for the enemy to come close or surround the defender.

For years the League of Nations and later the United Nations tried without success to define *aggressive* and *defensive*. Behind the search for definitions lay the idea that a defensive war was justified and an aggressive war was not. However, what seems to one nation to be aggressive is considered by another to be defensive and vice versa. The possibility that the Soviets may be developing an antimissile system, an avowedly defensive measure, has been interpreted by many American congressmen as a hostile gesture. James Reston carried this position to its logical conclusion in his column: "The Soviet Union has been the aggressor on this anti-missile madness." [14] A published interview with the director of a biological laboratory run by the University of California on contract to the U.S. Navy brought out the same offensive-defensive ambiguity. When asked if the laboratory's experiments could be involved with biological warfare, the director replied that he preferred to think of what his laboratory was doing as "defensive in nature," but he did not deny that the defensive side of biological research could be closely related to offensive uses in wartime situations.

The same sort of calculations can be made for spatial invasions as well as territorial defense under less ominous conditions, such as defending a table in a cafeteria or an adjacent empty seat on a bus. If one develops procedures that will keep away the timid invaders, the person most likely to occupy the space will be an aggressive boor. Would it be better to allow the seat to be occupied by the timid old lady who enters the bus first and who can be cowed by agonistic display than by an aggressive fellow who is likely to take additional space with his elbows and bundles? Are the 15 minutes of solitude worth the efforts of active defense plus the risks of an aggressive seatmate later? A person learns by experience the best method under various conditions and in rush hour is likely to use passive defense or retreat but to rely on active defense during the wee hours of the morning.

We conducted several studies to learn how offensive display and avoidance achieved spatial privacy. The first study used a three-page questionnaire, each page showing a diagram of a rectangular table with

[14] James Reston, "Billions Would Buy Rocket Defense But No Security," *The New York Times*, January 22, 1967, p. A5.

three, four, or five chairs per side. Twenty-four students were given
avoidance instructions, although the word itself was not used:

> If you wanted to be as far as possible from the distraction of other
> people, where would you sit?

Twenty-one students from the same class were shown the same diagram and given the *offensive display* instructions without the use of
that phrase:

> If you wanted to have the table to yourself, where would you sit to
> discourage anyone else from occupying it?

Even though both groups of students were asked to arrange themselves to gain privacy, the two tactics produced very different results
as far as the seats chosen (see Fig. 2). Those students who wanted
to sit by themselves as far as possible from other people overwhelmingly chose the end chairs. Those students who wanted to keep others
away from the table almost unanimously chose the middle chair.

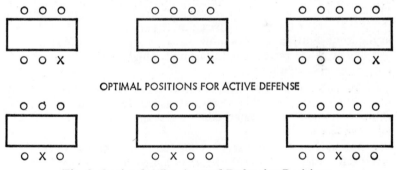

Fig. 2. Optimal Offensive and Defensive Positions.

When I sent an account of these findings to architect James
Marston Fitch, his first question concerned the location of the door.
Unfortunately, the diagrams showed a table and chairs floating in
space with no indication of where the door, other tables, or even the
walls were located. One hypothesis that came to mind was that someone attempting an offensive display would be likely to face toward the
door, whereas someone who was retreating would face the wall. It also
seemed likely that the back of the room would be more heavily used

by people in retreat. To explore these possibilities, another set of diagrams was drawn, each one showing a full room containing two rows of rectangular tables, aisles, and walls. Four sets of instructions, involving both retreat and active defense conditions as well as high and low room densities, were used with these diagrams.

HYPOTHESIS NO. 1. DURING THE RETREAT CONDITION PEOPLE WILL GRAVITATE TO THE END (WALL) CHAIR; IN ACTIVE DEFENSE THEY WILL MAKE GREATER USE OF THE CENTER AND AISLE CHAIRS. This hypothesis was strongly supported by the data. With the retreat instructions 76 per cent of the students chose a wall chair compared to 38 per cent during the active defense condition. Both the center chair and the aisle chair were chosen more frequently during active defense than during retreat.

HYPOTHESIS NO. 2. STUDENTS IN RETREAT WILL FACE AWAY FROM THE DOOR; DURING ACTIVE DEFENSE THEY WILL FACE TOWARD THE DOOR. The results show a general preference in all conditions to sit with one's back to the door—60 per cent of the total sample faced away from the door compared to 40 per cent who faced it. There was still a trend in the predicted direction since 44 per cent of the active defenders faced the door compared to 36 per cent of those in retreat.

Front versus rear of the room. In all conditions there was strong preference for chairs toward the rear of the room. Over-all, 79 per cent selected chairs at the rear compared to 21 per cent who selected chairs at the front. Further analysis showed that occupancy of the rear chairs was higher in the retreat conditions under high room density than in any of the other conditions.

Small versus large tables. There was a marked preference for the four-chair tables when they were paired with eight-chair tables, with 73 per cent selecting the small tables compared to 27 per cent selecting the large tables.

Tables against the wall versus tables with aisles on all sides. When given this choice, 62 per cent of the students selected the table against the wall compared to 38 per cent choosing a table with aisles on all sides.

Room density. When all those responses from the high density conditions were pooled and compared with all those from the low density conditions, there was no over-all difference. However, density interacted with several of the other variables and had more influence with the retreat instructions than with the active defense instructions. With high density and retreat instructions there was greater use of (1) the rear half of the room, (2) the tables against the wall, and (3) the chairs closest to the wall. It appears that the attribution of high room density increases the amount of physical retreat by those people who want to retreat, but has little effect on those who want to employ active defense.

As we have indicated, some areas are more suited to one tactic than the other. A large sociopetal room that orients everyone toward the center makes it difficult for people to retreat. Intimate living rooms as well as Indian tepees or Japanese huts built around a center hearth fall into this category. Conversely a large homogeneous area lacking lines of demarcation, barriers, or obstructions make it difficult to mark out and defend individual territories. Under most conditions, smaller well-articulated areas are easier to defend than large unobstructed areas. A person can defend a small cafeteria table up to the point at which almost all other tables are occupied, but the opposite end of a large table might be occupied by another individual or a couple even under conditions of low density. Our findings that the first occupant in these library study halls gravitated to end chairs indicates that avoidance positions are more widely used than offensive displays, which is probably related to the student's anticipation that future room density will be high. If we could locate a room in which density never exceeded one per table, we could expect to find more use of the central chair since it provides room on both sides of the person for writing and storage.

To learn something of territorial defense under conditions of high density, a study was conducted in a heavily used soda fountain on campus. This was a converted dormitory whose individual rooms were left intact, although the doors to the rooms were removed, ostensibly for ease of circulation, but also to prevent necking. Beverages, ice cream, and sandwiches were available in a central service area, and the students could then go outside on the porch or into any of eight side rooms. The procession of students walking down the hall searching for an empty room suggested the possibility of studying how a student might defend a room against intruders. An attractive 20-year-old girl who appeared to be studying was stationed at a table facing the door in one of the small rooms for 20-minute periods at various times during the week. On other days at the same hour the girl kept watch over the room from some distance away and recorded the number of people entering, where they sat, and how long they remained. The results showed that the student was *not* able to protect the room if an all-or-none criterion of outside occupancy was used. She was able to keep the room to herself in only one of the ten experimental sessions. The effect of her presence was noticeable only if one examined the seating of newcomers within the room. She was very successful in defending her own table. Over the ten experimental sessions only one student sat down at her table, and that occurred during a time of great crowding. This compared with a total of 13 students who occupied these chairs during the control sessions.

Territorial defense is not an all-or-none affair, even though it may be difficult under conditions of high density. Studies of birds have shown that at high densities territorial behavior is replaced by social rank behavior.[15] For studies of human crowding, a determined defense will mean not so much absence of intruders, but a gap between vacancy and occupation. A person sitting alone in a public cafeteria may be able to defend his table through agonistic displays at low or moderate densities, but he will almost certainly lose his exclusive domain at times of great crowding. An indication of his defensive prowess is seen in the fact that people refrain from sitting down at his table until all other tables are occupied and then make deferential gestures as they lower their trays and sit down.

People who remain in public areas for long periods—whether at a habitual chair at a weekly conference or on a commuter train—can establish a form of tenure. Their rights to this space will be supported by their neighbors even when they are not physically present. At a meeting it is not surprising to find a newcomer cautioned against sitting in a certain chair because it belongs to Smith even though it looks just like every other chair at the table. Ann Gibbs interviewed people in the campus soda fountain who habitually occupied the same tables. Their attitude that, "This is my table because I'm here all day," led her to develop an experiment in which people who had been seated for various lengths of time were approached and informed, "Excuse me, but you are sitting in my seat." Miss Gibbs found that people who had been seated for brief periods did not feel any rights to their chairs and moved away. However, those who had been seated for longer periods, strongly resisted the invasion. A short-timer replied hastily, "Oh, all right, excuse me—I'll move." He did not question the experimenter even though there were many vacant tables in the vicinity. However, when a fellow who had been seated for 25 minutes was told, "You are sitting in my seat," he replied, "No, I don't think so. I've been here a half-hour," and refused to move.[16]

We also studied the ways in which seats were reserved in several library study halls. Sally Robison recorded those objects that people used to reserve their seats while they were away. In libraries it was mainly books and coats, but in airports and bus stations one also found packages, briefcases, and umbrellas. She began experimental

[15] David E. Davis, "Territorial Rank in Starlings," *Animal Behaviour*, VII (1959), 214–21.

[16] R. Sommer and F. D. Becker, "Territorial Defense and the Good Neighbor" (Unpublished manuscript).

studies of territorial markers at times of relatively low room density—an average of two or three people at each 12-chair table, but was very discouraged about her "lack of results" since almost all the markers were effective. In 22 trials with markers ranging from notebooks to old newpapers, the territory was invaded only three times—twice when an old newspaper was used and once when a paperback book was left on the table. The implication is clear that at low densities almost any marker is effective in reserving space. One qualification is that the object must be perceived as a marker and not as litter. This requires the item either to have symbolic meaning as a territorial marker—a "Keep Out" or "Reserved" sign—or some intrinsic value—a coat, purse, or other object that the owner would not discard without cause. Specifically excluded would be items with no dollar value or symbolic importance—an empty matchbook, candy wrapper, or section from the previous day's newspaper. Certain forms of litter such as old newspapers or magazines may attract people to a given seat.[17]

Lee Mohr investigated the effectiveness of markers during high room density. He arrived at the study hall early in the evening, placed his territorial markers, and then departed to another table where he could observe. All the control (unmarked) areas were occupied well before the two-hour session had finished, the average time before occupancy being 20 minutes. Each of the markers delayed occupation, although some were more potent than others. A sport jacket and a notebooks-text-pen combination reserved the chair for the entire two-hour period. Magazines piled neatly in front reserved the chair for 77 minutes, whereas the same magazines randomly scattered kept it for 32 minutes. That the magazines were less effective markers than the textbook or the sport jacket is not surprising since they are non-personal objects that belong to the library and frequently remain on tables after people depart. There was an interesting sidelight on the role of the person adjacent to the marked space. In all five trials with the scattered magazines, the weakest marker of the five, the potential invader questioned "the person beside" as to whether the space were vacant. As a neighbor he is held responsible for knowing the status of the adjacent space. At first he unknowingly serves as the protector of the space and informs all potential invaders that he thinks the chair is taken. The belongings or journals left in the space indicate to him that the departed person is likely to return. As time passes he begins to doubt that the departed person will return and imparts this to potential invaders, "Yes, somebody was sitting there, but that was over an hour ago, maybe he's not coming back." Once the neighbor believes that the space has been deserted, he no longer feels obliged to protect it. Interestingly, no one questioned the neighbor when notebooks and the text were left on the table. With the sport jacket a few people asked if the seat were taken, and all save one (over 90 minutes after the trial began) were given affirmative answers and left the marked chair unoccupied.[18]

The neighbor's role in defending the property rights was also apparent in a study of home cage effects among laboratory reared and housed monkeys. Leary and Maroney found that a monkey's dominance position was lowered when he was a guest in another cage rather than a host. Since the cages were similar, it did not seem that the changed physical environment was responsible. When a new monkey was placed in a cage, both the host and the monkeys in adjacent cages engaged in aggressive, angry posturing, and vocalization toward the guest who appeared to be distracted and intimidated.[19] The role of the neighbor in protecting the adjacent space deserves further attention. We have a microcosm of a Property Owners Protective Association—the neighbor believing that he has to protect the marked chair lest he lose his own seat if he leaves the room himself. It might be possible to devise similar analogues to organized civic betterment and beautification. It should be possible to create noxious environmental situations that can only be ameliorated by the joint efforts of several occupants—for example, a table that is too close to an open window or too far away from available light sources. Institutional environments are generally accepted as sacred and immutable, but there may be conditions under which individuals spontaneously change them around. The most important factor may be a leader or simply an individual who does not respect the sanctity of the situation. Englishmen waiting patiently in bus queues will be grossly annoyed when someone walks directly to the front of the line, although they may tolerate him if he is a member of another culture where "they don't know about queues." People are generally held accountable for obeying norms that are not codified into law only if they are familiar with them. A person who alters a sacred institutional environment may be considered a hero fighting against bureaucracy or, more frequently, a cultural dunce who does not know any better.

A study of the good neighbor effect in a college library was undertaken by Frank Becker and Ralph Requa. Each session took place at

[18] Sommer and Becker, op. cit.

[19] R. W. Leary and R. J. Maroney, "The Effect of Home Cage Environment on the Social Dominance of Monkeys," Journal of Comparative and Physiological Psychology, LV (1962), 256–59.

six-chair tables, three chairs to a side, where there was a single male student at one end of the table with two chairs alongside him (O–O–X). The experimentor then sat at the other end chair on the same side (X–O–X) and after a designated interval (either five minutes or 15 minutes) left a stack of three paperback books and walked away. After either 20 or 60 minutes, the second experimentor entered the room and asked the neighbor if the marked chair was taken. The first finding was that none of the marked chairs was ever occupied by anyone else. All the markers were effective in holding the space under conditions of moderate room density. When we turn next to the neighbor's reaction to the question, we find that two-thirds of the neighbors defended the marked chair by saying, "Yes, this seat is taken" and one-third did not defend it. The length of time the former occupant had remained (5 or 15 minutes) had no effect on the neighbor's willingness to defend the chair. However, the length of time the previous occupant was absent had a significant effect. When the former accupant had been away 20 minutes, 80 per cent of the neighbors defended the chair but when he had been away 60 minutes, this fell to 54 per cent.[20]

Several aspects of the experiment require further elaboration. First of all, the former occupant had made no attempt to establish a relationship with the neighbor. It is an interesting hypothesis that a brief conversation—borrowing a match or asking the time—would have increased the neighbor's willingness to defend the space. Certainly it seems reasonable that the request "Save my chair while I'm gone" would have increased the neighbor's inclination to defend the space. However, it is still interesting that under the conditions studied to find that (a) a relatively impersonal marker was able to keep the space vacant, (b) the legitimacy of the marker was supported by two-thirds of all neighbors, and (c) the strength of the neighbor's defense was related to the length of time the former occupant had been away.

Territorial markers can be a serious management problem in public areas. Unless management forbids it and instructs some employee to specifically collect all coats and personal belongings draped over empty chairs, a third of the seats in a cafeteria can be out of use because of packages and coats left on the chairs to hold space for a person in line. The same practice will convert poolside chairs into towel racks. Because the principles governing reserved space in public areas are not explicit, they can be a source of friction. A lady enters the third row of a summer playhouse and sprawls her coat, handbag, and program over the adjacent six seats. Other patrons will begrudgingly respect her

---

[20] Sommer and Becker, *op. cit.*

territorial markers although they are not legally obliged to do so. It would be interesting to determine how far a person's domain can extend under these circumstances.

On the other hand, territoriality is accepted on airplanes during stopovers (one cannot usurp a seat that is marked "Occupied"), nor can a Las Vegas patron try a slot machine that has an "In Use" sign over it. There are numerous instances where management believes that it profits by giving customers individual areas. The obvious example is the reserved seat at a play or sports event. The creation of a fixed number of territories is also a common population-limiting device. This includes zoning laws which specify lot size for single family dwellings or per-acre density regulations for multiple-unit dwellings. Health and sanitation regulations are also used to keep population within prescribed limits.

Lack of understanding about spacing mechanisms is responsible for tables and desks intended to accommodate four or six persons per side (based on some arbitrary computation of square footage per person), but that appear "occupied" when one or two people sit there, or coffee rooms and lounges between floors in an office building or adjacent to the nurse's station in a hospital that become the private territory of a clique. It is fairly simple for one group of people to take over an area if they are the closest to it or otherwise have some inside track.

Many college officials have considered developing classrooms as multi-use space during evenings and weekends when classes are not in session. It seems wasteful to construct separate study halls when the classrooms remain empty so much of the time. Most such attempts have failed because of a lack of recognition of spacing mechanisms. In a survey of study facilities on five New England campuses, it was observed that the first student in a classroom became the *space owner* and subsequent students had to find empty rooms. A building that might have accommodated several hundred students would hold only 20 or 30.[21]

Both the good and the bad features of territoriality are apparent in this situation. First it provides, under normal conditions, a private area for each student, but it also restricts the number of students using the building to a figure below what college officials would regard as optimal. There are many who feel it is wasteful to keep a building open, pay for light, heat, and patrolling, when it is used by only a handful of students. There is no question but that territoriality produces waste (unoccupied) space, but it also confers certain benefits upon the owner—privacy, space to spread out and leave belongings,

[21] Stuart M. Stoke *et al., Student Reactions to Study Facilities* (Amherst: Committee on Cooperation, 1960).

and security about where his space ends and the next person's begins. What about those students who are unable to find rooms of their own— the hapless unterritoried flock? First they seek out an empty classroom and, not finding one, return to their rooms to study or use a public (nonterritorial) area in the library.

5

Small Group Ecology

A new cold war issue has developed: should the conference table be round or square? Round, said the Russians, square said the Western powers. . . . What was involved was the Western conception of the meeting as a four-power conference versus the Russian effort to bring in other nations. (*The New York Times*, May 17, 1959.)

GENERAL STUDIES

Social psychologists have long been troubled by the problem of defining a group. Definitions have ranged from the purely psychological, which do not require the physical presence of another person, exemplified by a study in which social influence was produced by recorded voices, to those involving physical presence without any social relationship between individuals. The systematic study of small groups is a comparatively recent development even in social psychology. For our purposes a group can be defined as a face-to-face aggregation of individuals who have some shared purpose for being together. The earliest studies in social psychology dealt with *social influence* or the way the presence of one person affected another. In 1897 Triplett noticed that a bicycle racer went faster when there was a strong competitor nearby. He brought this phenomenon into the laboratory by having people wind fishing reels in the presence of others and alone.[1] He found that

[1] N. Triplett, "The Dynamogenic Factors in Pacemaking and Competition," *American Journal of Psychology*, IX (1897), 507–33.

most people worked faster when someone else was present, a phenomenon known to track and field coaches whose teams will dull their abilities unless they have good competition. The improvement in performance resulting from the presence of other people was called a *social increment.* Later studies revealed that on certain tasks, particularly those calling for concentration and error-free performance, spectators and competitors often produced a decline in performance or *social decrement.*

It was not until the 1930's that intact groups were studied in the laboratory. Kurt Lewin and his associates developed concepts appropriate to the study of the group as an entity—leadership style, group cohesion, and group climate. In a now classic study they observed groups of boys making masks under the direction of democratic, authoritarian, or laissez-faire leaders.[2] The original results favored the democratic style of leadership, but it has taken 30 years to clarify these results. Now we know that democratic leadership isn't always the most efficient way of getting things done, particularly in cultures where there are strong authoritarian elements and people do not feel comfortable about discussing issues in public. Lewin developed the idea of the *life space,* the diagrammatic representation of all those forces affecting the individual at a given moment, and he believed that better predictions about a person's behavior could be made from knowing his life space than from knowing his situation as others would describe it. This emphasis on the individual's phenomenal world delayed the study of the physical environment since it seemed to emphasize psychological causation of behavior. Behavioristic psychology also slighted the study of the physical environment because of its preoccupation with laboratory studies and a reinforcement model of human behavior. The effects of environment are generally too diffuse and subtle to be explained by an animal pressing a lever to receive a food pellet. Few behaviorists have studied the effects of confinement per se on animal behavior, nor are they very knowledgeable about cage dimensions, isolated versus group animals, and so forth. These studies have generally been undertaken by people of a different philosophical persuasion, notably the ethologists who are just now regaining some of the influence they had exercised during the heyday of Darwinism.

Most social scientists still approach group behavior with the single-variable laboratory model. Thousands of research studies have produced considerable information about the behavior of college sophomores under artificial conditions. Much less is known about groups as they exist outside of the laboratory. Roger Barker has made the point

[2] Kurt Lewin, *A Dynamic Theory of Personality* (New York: McGraw-Hill Book Company, 1935).

that we know how children respond to the question, "What makes the clouds move?" without knowing how often children ask this question and under what circumstances it arises.[3] There is need for study of group processes from an ecological standpoint in which the adaptive value of aggregation can be seen and understood. In a pioneer investigation of group size, James and his students recorded the groupings they observed in two Oregon cities. They observed 7,405 informal groupings of pedestrians, playground users, swimmers, and shoppers, and 1,458 people in various work situations. They found that 71 per cent of all groups, both informal and work groups, contained only two individuals, 21 per cent contained three individuals, 6 per cent contained four, and 2 per cent contained five or more individuals.[4] These data make it abundantly clear that the size of the informal aggregation in these common situations is small indeed—consisting of two individuals most of the time. Our own cafeteria observations also indicate that informal groups of more than three individuals are rare. There is an urgent need for data on the point at which a larger aggregation tends to break up into smaller two-person and three-person subgroups. The point has some implication for the design of lounges and recreational facilities that cater to informal and spontaneous interaction. There is hardly a point in having conversational areas for groups of eight or ten unless there is some sort of structured activity involved.

Poets and artists lose no occasion to inform us that our age is marked by man's alienation from his neighbors. Paul Halmos illustrates how alienation is mirrored in changing dancing habits. Dancing began as a choral enterprise involving the entire community. It effectively served to share the burdens and deepen the bonds of fellow feeling as well as provide catharsis through rhythmic communal rapture. Choral dances were still practiced as late as the sixteenth and seventeenth centuries but no longer as the total communal experiences they had been. They were steadily replaced by couple dances in which the group was divided into independent couples. The cotillion-quadrille type of square dances represented a link between the choral and the couple dances. Halmos believed that the couple dance may still serve sexual and matrimonial purposes, but these are not necessarily communal purposes. The couples arrive *en deux* and rarely join others among the dancers.[5] Halmos' essay prepares us for the present fashion

[3] Roger G. Barker, "Explorations in Ecological Psychology, *American Psychologist*, XX (1965), 1–14.

[4] John James, "A Preliminary Study of the Size Determinant in Small Group Interaction," *American Sociological Review*, XVI (1951), 474–77.

[5] Paul Halmos, *Solitude and Privacy* (New York: Philosophical Library, Inc., 1953).

for young people to dance alone to the extent that it is difficult for a spectator to be certain which boy is which girl's partner. Touching of partners during the sound-drenched, light-drenched dances is taboo except at intermission when body contact between couples is universal. It would be interesting to see if an updating of James' study of natural groups would also disclose an increase in the number of lone individuals in public places.

As early as 1931, the sociologist Bogardus had stated, "It is only as social and physical facts can be reduced to, or correlated with, spatial facts that they can be measured at all." [6] However, the systematic study of spatial factors in face-to-face groups did not begin until 1950 with the study by Steinzor. As a leader of discussion groups, Steinzor had noticed one man change his seat in order to sit directly opposite another man with whom he had previously had a verbal altercation. Steinzor then went back through the past interaction records to see if group members were more likely to interact with people whom they could see. He found that when one person in the group finished speaking, it was the man opposite rather than someone alongside who was the next to speak.[7] Hearn found that the type of leadership within a group interacted with spatial effects to influence participation. With minimal leadership, people directed more comments to those sitting opposite (the Steinzor effect), but when a strong leader was present, people directed more comments to adjacent seats.[8] This illustrates the role played by eye contact in face-to-face groups. Based on the studies of dominance described earlier, we can hypothesize that with a strong leader close by, the individual restricts his gaze to adjacent seats, but when leadership is weak or absent, he can look anywhere and the stimulus value of people opposite becomes heightened.

Textbooks of group dynamics and applied psychology frequently allude to the idea that certain arrangements of people are more suited to certain activities than others. We decided to investigate this problem, not from the standpoint of specific practical tasks such as might occur in a work situation, but from that of certain attitudes (cooperation, competition, or separate action) and observe how people arranged themselves.

A. RECTANGULAR TABLES. Each student was asked to indicate his own seating and that of a friend on diagrams showing a rectangular table

[6] Emory S. Bogardus, *Contemporary Sociology* (Los Angeles: University of Southern California Press, 1931).

[7] Bernard Steinzor, "The Spatial Factor in Face-to-Face Discussion Groups," *Journal of Abnormal and Social Psychology*, XLV (1950), 552–55.

[8] Gordon Hearn, "Leadership and the Spatial Factor in Small Groups," *Journal of Abnormal and Social Psychology*, CIV (1957), 269–72.

(1–2–1–2). Students overwhelmingly chose a corner-to-corner or face-to-face arrangement for casual conversation (see Fig. 3). The explanations emphasized both physical proximity and visual contact in these arrangements. The students selected a side-by-side arrangement for cooperative activity and explained that it was easier to share things this way. Competing pairs generally chose face-to-face seating, although some used a distant seating pattern. Those who chose the face-to-face arrangement maintained that this stimulated competition. Various

PERCENTAGE OF Ss CHOOSING THIS ARRANGEMENT

Seating Arrangement	Condition 1 (conversing)	Condition 2 (cooperating)	Condition 3 (co-acting)	Condition 4 (competing)
X corner-to-corner	42	19	3	7
X___X (face-to-face)	46	25	32	41
diagonal corner	1	5	43	20
side opposite	0	0	3	5
X X side-by-side	11	51	7	8
distant ends	0	0	13	18
TOTAL	100	100	100	99

Fig. 3. Seating Preferences at Rectangular Tables.

distant or catty-corner arrangements were selected by students who worked separately at the same table (co-acting pairs). The students cited the minimal eye contact in a catty-corner arrangement—e.g.: "It allows staring into space and not into my neighbors face."

B. ROUND TABLES. A similar questionnaire was used with another group, except that a diagram showed round table surrounded by six chairs. Most pairs who wanted to converse or work together used adjacent chairs. Again the reasons emphasized psychological closeness: "I want to chat with my friend, not the whole cafeteria, so I sit next to her," and "more intimate, there are no physical barriers between us." The competing pairs chose to sit directly across from one another to keep from seeing each other's work, and to stimulate competition by being able to see how the other was doing. The students working separately left empty chairs between one another.

PERCENTAGE OF Ss CHOOSING THIS ARRANGEMENT

Seating Arrangement	Condition 1 (conversing)	Condition 2 (cooperating)	Condition 3 (co-acting)	Condition 4 (competing)
	63	83	13	12
	17	7	36	25
	20	10	51	63
TOTAL	100	100	100	100

Fig. 4. Seating Preferences at Round Tables.

C. PSYCHOLOGICAL INTIMACY. A question of some relevance in seating behavior is the psychological closeness of different arrangements. We asked groups of approximately 100 college students each in the United States, England, Holland, Sweden, and Pakistan to rate a series of 37 arrangements of pairs seated at square, round, and rectangular tables along a scale from "very intimate and psychologically close," to "very distant and psychologically remote." The rank order of closeness was identical in all five countries. Side-by-side seating was always the most intimate, followed by corner seating, face-to-face seating, and various distant or catty-corner arrangements.

D. DISTANCE AND INTIMACY. Russo asked students to rate diagrams of seating arrangements at a rectangular table (2–1–2–1). She found that increased distance produced ratings of less acquaintance, less friendliness, and lower talkativeness, except where increased eye contact counteracted the effects of increased distance. Even though the physical distance was greater between two people at the head and foot of the table, there was more psychological closeness between them than between people in a diagonal arrangement. The cultural influence of the head position was evident on the equality dimension. When one person was at the head of the table, the pair was considered less equal than if both members were at the ends of the table or both were at the sides.[9]

E. CHILDREN'S SEATING ARRANGEMENTS. An attempt was made to verify experimentally some of the questionnaire results from Studies A and B. We wanted to test children in cooperative competitive, and co-acting activities to determine how they would arrange themselves. Cooperating pairs sat side by side, competing pairs used a corner arrangement, and children working on separate tasks used a catty-corner arrangement. Very few children sat directly opposite one another, a widely used arrangement in studies of adults, second only in popularity to corner seating. It is likely that a 30-inch distance across the table was a much longer psychological distance on the children's scale than it would be for adults. As in previous studies, girls made more use than boys of side-by-side seating.[10] Elkin also found that sitting across was uncommon among young children but increased in frequency with age, while sitting side by side decreased with age.[11]

F. ADULT PAIRS. Since the previous study used children with a specific task, an additional study using adults with a different task seemed warranted. Each subject was told nothing about the task he was to perform, but only that his partner (or opponent) had already arrived

[9] Russo, op. cit.

[10] Gary Norum, Nancy Russo, and Robert Sommer, "Seating Patterns and Group Task," Psychology in the Schools, IV (1967), 276–80.

[11] Lorne Elkin, "The Behavioural Use of Space by Children" (Unpublished manuscript, 1964).

and was waiting in the experimental room. The room contained a large rectangular table (4–1–4–1), and the decoy always occupied the same chair—one from the end along the side of the table. The perceived relationship of cooperation or competition had a significant effect on seating. In the cooperative condition, 13 peple sat on the same side of the table as the decoy and 11 sat opposite. In the competitive condition, only four sat on the same side as the decoy, and 19 sat opposite. There was a trend, not statistically reliable, for females to make greater use of side-by-side seating.

G. Approval seating motives. Rosenfeld asked students to enter a room (in which a decoy was already seated) and to behave in such a way as to show the seated person that "you want to become friendly with her." Other subjects were told to imagine that the decoy was a girl they did not like and "you want to let her know that you don't want to become friendly with her." In both cases the subject was instructed not to come right out and tell the other person how he felt, but to communicate his feelings in other ways. The average distance the subject remained from the decoy in the approval-seeking condition was 57 inches, compared to an average of 94 inches in the avoidance condition.[12]

H. Discussion topic. Michael McNeill attempted to test the effects of discussion topics on seating arrangements at a rectangular table (1–3–1–3). Forty pairs of college girls were given topics that ranged from those very personal (Sex as Communication) to those that were relatively impersonal. The results showed that the topic made almost no difference in seating. Twenty pairs sat corner to corner, 12 sat opposite, and eight sat side by side[13] and this was composed of a perfect 5–3–2 for each of the four discussion topics. It seems apparent that it is the nature of the relationship between the individuals rather than the topic itself that characterizes a discussion as personal or impersonal. Two lovers discussing the weather can have an intimate conversation, but a zoology professor discussing sex in a lecture hall containing 300 students would be having an impersonal session regardless of the topic.

I. Personal space on long benches. Brian Talcott studied seating patterns at three 12-foot long benches at a Berkeley bus stop. Each bench could conceivably accommodate six people (allowing two feet per person), but it was typical to find two people, one at each end, "filling" the bench to the extent that other people would stand around

[12] H. M. Rosenfeld, "Effect of an Approval-Seeking Induction on Interpersonal Proximity," *Psychological Reports*, XVII (1965), 120–22.
[13] This ratio is similar to that found in our cafeteria studies. Cf. Sommer, 1959.

or sit on a nearby stone wall rather than occupy a center position. Mr. Talcott concluded that these long bus benches were inefficient and alternatives such as smaller sizes, or the introduction of armrests as barriers should be tested. As in the library, the first occupant of the bench gravitated to an end position, and the second occupant went to the opposite end. It is noteworthy that the sex of the person seated at the other end of the bench was irrelevant to the second occupant. A male was just as likely to sit down at one end of the bench with a female at the other end as when a male was at the other end.[14] The lack of any sexual segregation indicates that the incumbent was able to remain a nonperson. Although this can be considered a desirable feature from the standpoint of maintaining privacy, the efficiency of 12-foot benches that accommodate a maximum of two people can be questioned.

J. THE LIMITS OF COMFORTABLE CONVERSATION. This study was based on the previous observation that people conversing prefer to sit across from one another, although at some slight angle, rather than side by side. However, it is obvious that this must be qualified by the size of the gap between the people. If two men are given the choice of conversing across from one another at a distance of 30 feet or sitting side by side on a sofa, they will select the sofa. This means that people will sit across from one another until the distance between them exceeds the limit for comfortable conversation. By noting the point at which people begin to sit side by side, we can learn the limits of comfortable conversation under the particular conditions used. Two sofas in an attractively furnished lounge were placed at prearranged distances from one another before each session. Pairs of subjects were asked to enter the lounge and discuss various impersonal topics. Table 1 shows that when the couches were placed one to three feet apart, people sat opposite one another. This does not mean they sat directly opposite one another since one person may have sat on the left side of one couch whereas the other sat on the right side of the other couch. However, the people did sit on different couches. From three-and-one-half feet and beyond, people sat side by side. It can be noted that, with couches like these, people's heads are usually one foot behind the front of the couch. Using the architect's concept of nose-to-nose distance, our subjects began to sit side by side when they were five-and-one-half feet apart. Under the particular conditions we used—two people who knew each other slightly discussing an impersonal topic in a large lounge—this can be considered the upper limit for comfortable conversation. In many private homes, however, conversational

[14] See Footnote 20, Chapter 3.

distance is much longer. One difference is the room scale is smaller in private homes, and there is some evidence that as room size becomes larger, people sit closer together. The same occurs when noise level and distraction increase.

Table 1. Seating with Couches at Varying Distances.

Distance between couches in feet	Number of pairs sitting	
	Across	Side by side
1	8	4
2	11	2
3	12	6
3.5	1	8
4	1	11
5	2	8
6	0	5

K. Conversational distance side by side and across. The couches used in Study J permitted distance across to be varied systematically. It seemed desirable to conduct a further investigation in which four chairs were substituted for the two couches, which meant that the side-by-side distance could be varied, too. If people are given a choice between sitting five feet apart and across from one another *or* five feet apart but alongside one another, how will they sit? The results support the idea that people who want to converse will sit across from one another rather than side by side. However, the preference for sitting opposite is true only when the distance across is equal to or less than the side-by-side distance. When the distance across was greater than the distance side by side, most pairs sat side by side (see Table 2).

Table 2. Seating with Four Chairs at Varying Distances.

	Number of pairs sitting	
	Across	Side by side
Distance across = side-by-side distance	16	3
Distance across < side-by-side distance	35	1
Distance across > side-by-side distance	12	24

L. Conversational and co-acting groups. On one college campus, we found a cafeteria that served a number of different functions. During meal hours it was a crowded eating place, but between meals it was a half-empty lounge and study place for assorted students and employees. This made it possible to study spatial arrangements in the same setting by people who were eating, conversing, or studying. The observations took place over a one-year period during nonmeal hours, and a distinction was made between people who were interacting (conversing or studying together) and those who were co-acting (occupying the same table but studying or drinking coffee separately). At the small square tables, interacting pairs showed a definite preference for corner seating, whereas co-acting pairs sat opposite one another. At the rectangular tables interacting pairs preferred corner seating and, to a lesser extent, opposite seating. However, more than two-thirds of the co-acting pairs chose distant arrangements that separated the two people spatially and visually.

Table 3. Arrangement of Pairs in Student Cafeteria.

Seating arrangement	Per cent conversing pairs (N = 74)	Per cent coacting pairs (N = 18)
Corner	54	0
Across	36	32
Side	6	0
Distant	4	68

DISCUSSION AND IMPLICATIONS

We have seen that the spacing of individuals in small groups is not random but follows from the personality and cultural backgrounds of the individuals involved, what they are doing, and the nature of the physical setting. Stated more simply, we can say that spatial arrangements in small groups are functions of personality, task, and environment. Anthropologist Edward Hall has described how people from different countries interpret the language of space. What Americans experience as crowded, Latin Americans may perceive as spacious. A Latin American official who gave Hall a tour of a factory remarked, upon opening the door of an 18 × 20 foot office that contained seventeen clerks at individual desks, "See, we have nice spacious offices. Lots of space for everyone." Furniture in the American's home is placed around the edges, but the Japanese family gather in the middle of the room. An American in the Middle East or Latin America is likely to feel crowded and hemmed in—people come too close, lay their hands on him, and crowd against his body. He doesn't feel this in England or Scandinavia where it is the American who perceives the local residents as cold and aloof.[15] Small group ecology is particularly suited to cross-cultural studies since spatial arrangement can be easily and reliably recorded using inexpensive photographs as well as diagrams and moving pictures, and such recordings do not depend on the use of language or extensive familiarity with the culture. Questionnaires using diagrams and drawings with minimum reliance on language are also practicable. Whether there are general principles of spacing that apply in most cultures is an interesting question. Humans everywhere have a similar arrangement of sense organs, although they may use them differently. Since our eyes are at the front of our heads, since we have simple rather than compound eyes, and since we locate things spatially by sound as well as sight, certain consistencies in spatial arrangements could arise regardless of culture. On the other hand, Westerners are communicating to an increasing extent by telephone, letter, and teletype, which frees interaction from spatial constraints.[16]

Personality differences as distinct from cultural factors have been the subject of less investigation. Several studies have shown that introverts remain further away from other people than do extroverts, which is another way of saying that spatial distance as well as social distance are aspects of what we call introversion.[17] Fear of rebuke tends to increase individual distance but approval seeking reduces it. A shared fear such as that produced by a ghost story reduces social distance,[18] and it seems probable that internal threat—some danger originating within the group itself—would increase the average spatial distance between individuals. The most extreme form of withdrawal from other people is manifested by schizophrenic individuals who are fearful of being

[15] Edward T. Hall, *The Hidden Dimension* (Garden City, New York: Doubleday & Company, Inc., 1966).

[16] Most of these studies have been concerned with the arrangement of people vis-à-vis one another rather than with respect to barriers, borders, and boundaries. There is a line of research typified by the work of de Jonge that has focused on the way people arrange themselves in parks, recreational areas, and buildings. He has found a preference for areas that are marked, bounded, and make possible visual contact with surrounding areas. Other studies by de Jonge in Dutch railway stations, cafeterias, and reading rooms show clearly that people gravitate to wall locations that have privacy and the opportunity for visual contact with the outside in preference to exposed tables in central areas. See Derk de Jonge, "Applied Hodology," *Landscape,* XVII (Winter 1967–68), 10–11.

[17] Williams, *op. cit.;* Leipold, *op. cit.*

[18] S. Feshbach and N. Feshbach, "Influence of the Stimulus Object upon the Complementary and Supplementary Projections of Fear," *Journal of Abnormal and Social Psychology,* LXVI (1963), 498–502.

hurt in social intercourse. Our studies have shown that they not only remain too far from others but on occasions come too close.[19] This was particularly evident in decoy studies in which male and female schizophrenics sat immediately alongside a male decoy whom they knew slightly or not at all, which happened rarely if ever among the normal group. This behavior on the part of the schizophrenic violates the personal space of others who become offended by his excessive closeness. One can speculate on whether this relates to the schizophrenic's lack of a stable self-image and clear self-boundaries. A person unsure of who he is may not be clear as to where he ends and the next person begins.

Kleck and his associates have undertaken an interesting series of studies on the effect of stigma upon interaction distance. College students were asked to go into a room and converse with another person who was sometimes described as an epileptic. They sat further from the other person when he was described as an epileptic than when he was not. The experiment was repeated with the other person described either as "warm and friendly" or "cold and unfriendly." It was found that people sat further away from the "unfriendly" person than from the "friendly" person.[20] A further study was done to learn how far people would remain from an amputee. In this case a young man in a specially adapted wheel chair simulated the amputee. College students were asked to enter the room and teach either the amputee or a normal person to fold paper figures. The students sat further from the amputee than from a supposedly normal individual.[21] These studies were supported by grants from an association to aid crippled children, which was interested in exploring the isolation experienced by stigmatized individuals. The fact that a person in a wheel chair is kept at a greater distance would be likely to have some effect upon his motivation, attitudes, and feelings of belonging with normal individuals.

There is a definite need for studies of the ecology of natural work groups, not only as a complement for laboratory studies, but from the standpoint of determining how task affects physical arrangements. Whyte studied the ecology of 12 Chicago restaurants where friction between the dining room and the kitchen employees was commonplace. He attributed some conflict to the role reversal that occurred when female waitresses handed orders to male cooks who were more

[19] Sommer, 1959, *op. cit.*

[20] Robert Kleck, "Physical Stigma and Task Oriented Instructions," *Human Relations,* in press.

[21] Robert Kleck *et al.,* "The Effect of Stigmatizing Conditions on the Use of Personal Space," *Psychological Reports,* in press.

highly paid and skilled than the waitresses. Whyte found the difficulty could be resolved by eliminating direct face-to-face contact between waitresses and cooks.[22] Some restaurants reduce the friction by having the waitresses place the customers' orders on slips that are attached on a clipboard to the window between kitchen and dining room. The men pick off the order slips, fill them, and put the plates in the compartment where the waitresses pick them up, thus eliminating all face-to-face contacts. In the code of the American West, a face-to-face encounter constituted a challenge that could not be ignored. The prudent man stepped aside when the top guns walked down the street. Dwight Eisenhower describes this code in a speech delivered in November 1953:

> I was raised in a little town . . . called Abilene, Kansas. We had as our Marshall a man called Wild Bill Hickok. Now that town had a code, and I was raised as a boy to prize that code. It was: Meet anyone face-to-face with whom you disagree. You could not sneak up on him from behind, or do any damage to him, without suffering the penalty of an enraged citizenry. If you met him face-to-face and took the same risks as he did, you could get away with almost anything, as long as the bullet was in front.[23]

The studies described here tell us many things about the way that people in face-to-face groups, predominately Americans, use space. It will only be a matter of time before comparable studies of other cultures begin to appear in the literature. Certainly the work of Hall and Birdwhistell augurs well in this regard. However, it is important to ask how these findings can be applied in practice—how they can be marketed to do some good and increase the sum total of human happiness. If one finds that French Canadian students are able to tolerate closer presence than can their English Canadian counterparts, does this mean that a Quebec architect can (a) use a smaller room for the same number of students, (b) double the number of students in ordinary size classrooms, or (c) attempt to change the students' spatial preferences by increasing the distances between chairs? The answers must be given in terms of goals, objectives, and values rather than technical specifications. The architect can develop the present trends even further—take advantage of the closeness of French-Canadian students and use smaller classrooms—or make the classroom more sociofugal in order to keep the students away from one another—or

[22] W. F. Whyte, *op. cit.*
[23] Robert A. Aurthur, review of *The Western Hero,* in *The Nation* (January 24, 1966), p. 107.

he can disregard this finding completely. What he *should* do is a question of value that involves something which he creates himself or accepts from others; it does not flow out of the problem itself. It is possible to treat symmetry and harmony as absolute values and arrange the classrooms in terms of a spatial esthetic under the assumption that schoolchildren are exceedingly plastic and should be molded in line with universal and logical spatial principles. I prefer to begin with the idea that man himself and what he wants to do (his value system) represents the yardstick by which design solutions must be measured.

This still leaves open the question of how studies of *what is* can help in deciding *what should be*. These two conditions are not necessarily independent; what presently exists tends to become sacred (i.e., valuable in its own right). A designer is rarely criticized for doing what has been done in the past; he may not get much praise for it either, but there will be few cries of indignation or outrage. There are reasons—historical, cultural, economic, and functional—why things developed as they did. The schoolhouse is not simply the result of accident and inadequate theorizing; it arose in response to a certain type of teaching (sit and learn) in a certain type of society. Studying the nature of nature has always been an important part of any scientific field although one finds it occasionally labeled as a preliminary or "pre-experimental" activity.

Observational data can also be used in teaching people who must work in various settings. An English-Canadian teacher may feel uncomfortable at the close proximity of her French-Canadian pupils and her French-Canadian colleagues. Not being aware that this is part of their culture, she may feel personally affronted and assaulted—on the edge of panic. The Jewish child from New York's lower East Side where close contact is the rule is likely to feel that people in the Midwest are cold and distant. Apart from the idea of designing schools for Puerto Rican or Jewish children that take into account the way these children use time and space—and I want to emphasize that I am not sure how this can be done—there seems the more practical possibility of using knowledge of the ethnic group to prepare teachers from other backgrounds who will work with the children. One teaches *what is* to people who must deal with the present situation rather than, in the case of building a school for X group of children, equating what is with what should be.

From a practical standpoint, knowledge of how groups arrange themselves can assist in fostering or discouraging relationships. A library that is intended to be sociofugal space, where interaction is discouraged, requires knowledge of how to arrange people to minimize unwanted contact. One possibility is to use the rank order of preferred arrangements by interacting groups as arrangements to be avoided in sociofugal space. On this basis, corner seating would be less satisfactory than opposite or distant seating in the sociofugal setting. An Emily Post or Amy Vanderbilt may know these principles intuitively, and diplomatic protocol may codify them, but there is need to make them explicit and subject them to empirical test. To an increasing extent we find ourselves being arranged by impersonal environments in lecture halls, airports, waiting rooms, and lobbies. Many aspects of the proximate environment have been placed for ease of maintenance and efficient cleaning with little cognizance given to their social functions. These principles will be of most help in institutional settings where the occupants have little control over their surroundings. The study of small group ecology is important, not only from the standpoint of developing an adequate theory of human society that takes into account the context of social relationships, but also from the practical standpoint of designing and maintaining functional spaces where human relationships can develop.

PART TWO

Special Settings

We turn now to four different man-environment systems—the mental hospital, school, tavern, and college dormitory. They are all institutional settings intended to illustrate the relationship between diverse and sometimes opposed groups of people, the physical environment, and administrative rules and traditions. The settings are selected for their differences rather than for any recurring theme. The mental hospital is a setting where the people are relatively passive and helpless in the face of an environment that is arranged for them with the goal of therapy in mind. The school is an institution devoted to learning but designed for a particular model of teaching (sit and learn) that many educators feel is outmoded. The influence of the custodians upon spatial arrangements is evident in both the school and the mental hospital. The tavern is used to illustrate the importance of laws and regulations in understanding why buildings are designed as they are. Perhaps there is no other building form in American society where the influence of legal regulations is so evident. The college dormitory is the first of these settings where the culture of the users emerges as a potent force in the design specifications. Unlike most mental patients, schoolchildren, and tavern patrons, college students have leasehold arrangements for their rooms and adapt these rooms to suit their individual needs. The two concluding chapters focus upon the rationale of environmental programming and the potential contribution of behavioral science to the design fields.

6

Designed for Refuge and

Behavior Change

There were wards upon wards of patients sitting in idleness, day after day, and retreating farther and farther into their private worlds until they were, it seemed, completely out of touch with reality. (Albert Deutsch, *The Mentally Ill in America*)

THE LADIES CONVERSE

My interest in environmental engineering dates from the time an internist for an elderly ladies' ward at a state hospital asked for help in discovering what was wrong with the place. Several thousand dollars had been spent to improve the ward—curtains framed the windows, the reflection of fluorescent lights danced on the new tile floor, tubular steel chairs with brightly colored plastic seats gave a Mondrian touch to the walls, and several air conditioners guarded the windows. The renovation is instructive since it reveals what can happen when people discover money. The old folks' ward was located in Western Canada where extensive federal, provincial, and local welfare programs were in force. In the 1950's a bright civil servant deduced that inmates of institutions were indeed citizens and eligible for federal old age pensions. Seventy-five dollars a month may seem small in absolute terms, but it was a great windfall to all players in the institutional game—custodians, patients, and relatives—since the pensions had accumulated over the years. Some patients had comfortable nest eggs when they were discharged, but if a patient died at the institution, his estate, including the accumulated pension funds, went to his relatives. At this particular hospital the administration decided to spend some pension funds on amenities for the elderly.

New furniture, air conditioners, and a television set were purchased for the ward. There is no record of what the ladies said about the change since no one solicited their opinions before or after. This is the customary state of affairs in custodial institutions where, in return for the beneficence of free room and board, the grateful inmates are expected to accept their environment as it is. The patients have privileges rather than rights, visitors instead of families. This became painfully evident when I interviewed patients about their wards. The patients were taken by surprise, and the nurses were suspicious. Of course, no one had solicited their opinions about the renovations either. The changes were planned and initiated from above, and completed by people who spent no time on the ward. The floor tiles, for example, were all the same pattern and ran the same way, which made the large lounge look even larger and more institutional than it had before. This singular style was not due to deliberate planning or economy but stemmed from inertia and the inability to realize that floor designs (or the color scheme or chair arrangement) made any difference. Most items were purchased and positioned for ease of maintenance rather than comfort or therapy. Occasionally the outcome bordered on the bizarre from the standpoint of human relationships. Most of the chairs on this ward stood in straight lines along the walls, but there were several rows back-to-back in the center; around several columns there were four chairs, each chair facing a different direction! The tragedy was not that these arrangements existed but that they were accepted as normal and reasonable throughout the institution. To compound the irony, pictures of this ward before and after the renovation formed a major portion of the hospital's application for an improvement award. The pictures revealed such a dramatic improvement in the physical conditions of the ward that the hospital won its award easily.

Despite the good publicity, the ward physician was dissatisfied with the outcome, although he could not specify his reasons. The ward looked better, but the ladies' mental state was unchanged. We visited the ward together, and I took to sitting there alone on long afternoons. Initially I shared his enthusiasm for the new furnishings. There was no denying that it was the best furnished ward in the hospital; as such it was regarded as somewhat of a model to be seen by visitors on tour. It took several weeks of sitting and watching before I could sort figure from ground and see what was not happening as well as what was. With as many as 50 ladies in the large room, there were rarely more than one or two brief conversations. The ladies sat side by side against the newly painted walls in their new chrome chairs and exercised their options of gazing down at the newly tiled floor or looking up at the new fluorescent lights. They were like strangers in a train station waiting for a train that never came. This shoulder-to-shoulder arrangement was unsuitable for sustained conversation even for me. To talk to neighbors, I had to turn in my chair and pivot my head 90 degrees. For an older lady, particularly one with difficulties in hearing and comprehension, finding a suitable orientation for conversation was extremely taxing. I hardly need add that there was no conversation whatever between occupants of the center chairs that faced different directions.

In retrospect, the reasons for the straight-row arrangement are not difficult to understand. First, there is the lack of explicit principles relating furniture arrangement to social intercourse. Sensitive individuals intuitively know that there is a connection, and people who want to converse will, consciously or unconsciously, occupy chairs with a suitable orientation and distance, but this is on a prescientific and nonverbal basis, something that is unlikely to play much part in the bureaucratic intricacies of institutional architecture. Magazines in medical specialities and allied fields devote considerable space to hospital construction and ward design, but the published plans and blueprints reveal only bare walls and rooms. The arrangement of furniture is left to the ward staff who do not realize the therapeutic potential of furniture arrangements. Ward geography is taken for granted, and a chair becomes something to sweep around rather than a necessary tool for social interaction. The same criticism has been leveled at American playgrounds by Lady Allen who pioneered the "adventure playground" in Great Britain. She described the American playground as "an administrator's heaven and a child's hell . . . asphalt barracks yards behind wire screen mesh barriers," built primarily for ease and economy of maintenance.

The inadequacy of the ward arrangement was also apparent when we contrasted it, not only with the conversational groupings in private homes, but also with the arrangement in the corridor outside the ward. Because of the absence of special visiting rooms (space was short and patients' families had a low priority in the competition for available space), this corridor was used by families and friends during visiting hours. Before the building opened to the public at 8:00 a.m., the custodian arranged the chairs in straight rows shoulder to shoulder against the walls. Several hours later relatives had moved the chairs into small groups so that they could face one another and converse comfortably. This was the typical situation in the corridor, but it *never* occurred on the ward. It was clear that families and friends arranged their environment to suit their needs, but the patients were being arranged by it.

Certain arrangements of furniture are very efficient from the standpoint of ward chores. It is a sad commentary that more is known about this aspect of furniture arrangement than about its therapeutic use. Nurses often complain about a ward that looks "junky" or cluttered. A quasi-military arrangement of chairs in neat rows along the wall appears neater, besides making it easier to sweep and survey the ward at a glance. It takes only a second to look down a continuous row of chairs against the wall, compared with the several seconds required to survey a cluttered room with an irregular seating pattern. Placing chairs along the walls left wide pathways for foodcarts and cleaning wagons to pass freely. Food service personnel and maintenance employees often came through this ward because of ease in transit. The large highway converted the ladies' living space into corridor space that could not be occupied without the risk of injury from the express traffic passing through.

Another factor responsible for the straight-row arrangement was the "institutional sanctity" that prevails whenever people spend long periods of time in any environment. After a time, no matter how unusual or unpleasant it seemed at first, the customary becomes fixed and natural. This can apply to the deafening noises of an auto assembly plant as well as the straight-row classrooms in schools. Hospitals, too, have a way of seeming right and efficient to their inhabitants, no matter how they appear to outsiders. In the old folks' ward, the staff no longer noticed the odors and clanking of keys that bothered visitors. The same was true of hospital routines, including the fact that patients were awakened every morning at 5:30. The old-line attendants who were the moral arbiters of the hospital had decreed that the night shift had a "soft touch" and so should bear the additional responsibility of getting the ladies dressed and ready for breakfast before the day shift arrived. Since there were 83 ladies on the ward who averaged 74 years of age and only two nurses on the graveyard shift, this meant starting early in order to get everyone up. The first ladies up and dressed waited two hours until the day shift arrived and served breakfast. Knowing this, it is not difficult to understand why the ladies were tired and ready for bed at 7:00 p.m. This time schedule produced awkward results when several ladies left the ward to live outside. It was the goal of social service to place as many of the ladies as possible in private homes in the belief that from the patient's standpoint as well as the cost to the state, this was preferable to living in an institution. Several ladies had to return to the hospital because people objected to their rising at 5:30 a.m. only to sit in the living room waiting for breakfast. Going to bed at 7:00 p.m. did not endear them to households where courtesy dictated a minimum of noise and disturbance while someone sleeps.

The effects of institutional sanctity are most pernicious for individuals who are infirm, helpless, or passive. For schizophrenic people, whose withdrawal and passivity can be compounded by disturbances of perception and thinking, objects may appear fixed and immutable or charismatic and magical. The pattern of a chair may have a symbolic meaning and a patient will not sit down until he has performed a special ritual. There may be gross perceptual distortions of size and distance that affect his view of the environment in addition to secondary disturbances of hospitalism, institutionalitis, and disculturation resulting from living in a large impersonal institution. It is common to find inmates whose original symptoms have abated, but who have become maladapted to life outside. Inmates and keepers alike come to accept routine as sacred and stability as an absolute value. When we tried to rearrange ward furniture, we encountered patients (and nurses, too) who considered it their duty to correct any deviation from "the way things belonged." After cleaning time, it was surprising to see how quickly furniture returned to its original location. This attitude was described by Jane Hillyer who spent eight years as a mental patient.

> I also assumed a slight proprietary attitude towards the cottage. After I had dusted that table about fifty times it became my table. It was my task to keep it in order, see that it had flowers on it, and a fresh cover, see that things were not left around, that books were kept in fairly neat piles, and knitting left in its proper bag. Woe to the offender! [1]

Individual patients mark out territories on the ward, and any territorial violation produces disturbance. That the nursing staff come to accept the territorial boundaries set by patients is one of the chief impediments to close staff-patient contact. Typically one finds the nurses driven back to a small area around their station. This is nonverbal and inexplicit, but an impressionist painting of a mental ward would show patches of white around the nurses' station surrounded by a sea of blue and gray representing the patients in their drab clothing. When I sat in the dayroom making observations, not only did patients and staff feel uncomfortable to see me there, but I felt personally unwanted. Robert Pace, an anthropologist, spent considerable time charting the location of patients and staff in a veterans' hospital. He found that the attendants were seen near the entrance of the

[1] Jane Hillyer, *Reluctantly Told* (New York: The Macmillan Company, 1931), p. 117.

dayroom three times as often as they were in the middle or rear of
the room. When questioned, the attendants explained that if they
lingered in the rear, "it upset the boys back there," but "you can
talk to these men here." Pace described how the patients' nonverbal
cues as to space ownership forced him back into the "staff area." On one
occasion he was hit by a patient when he unwittingly occupied the
patient's chair.

> For the next few days I change chairs a number of times in response
> to very apparent cues, such as increased verbal hallucinations or ritual-
> istic behaviors—apparent because my presence or absence brought imme-
> diate increases or decreases in their frequency. Gradually my comfortable
> living space was confined to that of the aides although I had hoped to
> avoid identification with other personnel. The means of communicating
> living space was almost entirely by what is commonly seen as psychotic
> behavior.[2]

The existence of "favorite chairs" is a typical feature of institutional
life. In interviews with staff and residents in 17 English old folks'
homes, Lipman found the "habitual occupation of particular chairs"
in each institution. Over 90 per cent of those patients who regularly sat
in the sitting rooms occupied the same chairs in the same positions each
day. Attendants and domestics located the residents in relation to their
favorite chairs. Furthermore, when anyone assisted a patient to and
from the sitting room, he was invariably told by the person himself
or by neighbors where "X's chair" was in the room. It was clear that
both nurses and other residents by their behavior reinforced the system of chair ownership. This situation was a source of great confusion
to newly admitted patients who had difficulty locating an unowned
chair. Sometimes a new resident would be driven from seat to seat until
he found one that did not belong to anyone. Interestingly, in their administrative rules and official statements, the nursing staff attempted
to discourage space ownership. Senior welfare officials and the matrons
of the homes claimed that this policy was intended to avoid feelings
of favoritism and possessiveness among the residents and to encourage
them to "mix with the others." However, as we have mentioned, the
behavior of the nurses in reinforcing the ownership system as well
as the inmates' desires for places of their own undermined the official
policy, which was ignored in practice.[3]

[2] Robert E. Pace, "Situational Therapy," *Journal of Personality*, XXV (1957),
578–88.

[3] Alan Lipman, "Territorial Behavior in the Sitting Rooms of Four Residential
Homes for Old People," *British Journal of Geriatric Practice*, in press.

The hospital administrator who does not arrange his wards to facilitate interaction will find the wards arranging the patients to minimize it. Here is an account written by a schizophrenic girl as she neared recovery:

> To the stupefaction of the nurse, for the first time I dared to handle the chairs and change the arrangement of the furniture. What unknown joy to have an influence on things; to do with them what I liked, especially to have the pleasure of wanting the change. Until now I had tolerated no change, even the slightest. Everything had to be in order, regular, symmetrical. That night I slept very well.[4]

Before undertaking our experiment, we spent some time observing seating patterns in a variety of places—homes, bus depots, railway stations, theaters, and hotel lobbies. We became aware of how incorrect our assumptions about public places had been. We had naively believed that hotel lobbies and railway stations were full of people sitting and talking. In actuality, most people sat alone reading or looking at new arrivals. People who were talking invariably had arrived together. People who came alone sat alone and did not interact at all. This provided very little precedent for developing institutional architecture that would bring the residents of this old folks' home into greater contact with one another. The resort hotel might have provided a suitable model, but the clientele usually is young, active, and eager for new friends and social activities in contrast to our own population of elderly men and women incarcerated, often against their will. Organized games or musical activities might have brought younger people together, but our ladies were, if not infirm, at least sedentary. After reviewing the various possibilities, we decided that the ladies would be more likely to converse if they sat facing one another rather than shoulder to shoulder. Our initial view (which was modified later) was that the people should be pointed towards one another like projectiles in order to maximize conversation. We also felt that the large open areas should be broken into smaller spaces, so that each person could select one or two others with whom to interact. Partitions might have served our purpose, but we decided to start with small tables placed around the ward. This upset the highway patrol no end, since they now had to navigate food carts and cleaning wagons around the tables instead of the long open stretch that they had before. Several of the nurses remarked that the tables made the ward look "junky." It seemed reasonable that we should give the ladies these islands of

---

[4] Marguerite Sechehaye, *Autobiography of a Schizophrenic Girl* (New York: Grune & Stratton, Inc., 1951), p. 80.

security around which they might group their chairs. We felt that the ladies would feel uncomfortable if their chairs were out in the oceanic spaces. Square tables have the advantage of letting a person know the boundaries of his territory. This seemed an important consideration for an older person whose sole personal area might be the table space in front of her. With round tables a person never knows where his territory ends and another's begins.

The dayroom was a large open area that, prior to the study, contained 43 chairs, four couches, and four small tables. The tables were placed out in the center of the room, too far from the chairs to be useful, and were employed only for formal activities and for patients whose special diets required them to eat separately. For two weeks prior to the beginning of the study, we recorded all interaction that took place in the dayroom. At various times of the day an observer visited the ward and recorded everything that happened during five-minute periods. So little interaction took place on the ward that longer sessions added little new information. Anything that occurred was recorded on mimeographed floor plans.

After two weeks we removed three of the old couches and introduced five additional square tables (30 inches per side), making a total of nine tables. The chairs were moved away from the walls and placed around the tables in various parts of the room. The first two weeks following the change was a stabilization period and no interaction counts were taken. During this time the nurses encouraged the ladies to sit at the tables. On the morning when the ladies first discovered the change there were spontaneous comments such as, "Where is our chesterfield? We miss our chesterfield." "This is a nice table, but I don't want to eat all day." and "Is this my chair now?" The last comment reflects the fact that individual chairs were moved to new locations. The maintenance and food service employees complained loudly that the tables and chairs cluttered their route through the ward. An occupational therapist inquired whether we were getting ready to hold a party.

It soon became apparent that if we wanted the ladies to remain at the tables, we would have to make the new locations more attractive. Put another way, we had to give the ladies some reasons for remaining at the tables. We hoped that this would become less necessary as the advantages of the tables for social intercourse became evident. We had imagined that the ladies would initially resist a new furniture arrangement and endeavored to counteract this by associating the tables with pleasant experiences and objects. Artificial flowers and vases were placed on the tables (later, real flowers were used) and magazines were laid out every day. Even so, it was difficult to persuade the ladies to remain at the tables. The ladies moved their chairs back against the walls at every opportunity. Indeed the movement of chairs back to the walls continued for some years afterwards and seems to have important psychological significance. Later studies of seating patterns of groups of people, both healthy individuals and patients of various sorts, also showed that people like to sit with their backs to walls and other tangible barriers. Part of this is simply because of comfort and the possibility of leaning one's chair back against a solid surface, but there also seems to be a need for security.

A wall location facing out enables one to see what is going on. In a barren institutional environment, this is exceedingly important, since the most exciting events are people coming and going. A good vantage point can provide advance information on meals, medication trays, and craft periods. When we mapped room density, we found that the highest concentrations of persons occurred in the small corridor at the entrance to the dayroom. Further observation and interviewing disclosed three major factors responsible for the high density: the certainty of seeing visitors to the ward from this location, its proximity to the dining hall, and the fact that the corridor contained the only windows low enough to permit an outside view.

Our primary concern was to see whether the new arrangement would increase interaction between the ladies. The record sheets distinguished between transient verbal interaction (asking a question, shouting at another patient, extending a greeting) and sustained verbal interaction (reciprocated conversations maintained over two seconds). Because of the difficulty of deciding what constituted nonverbal interaction (touching hands or giving food), recording was limited to verbal interaction between patients. Table 4 shows the results of observations made before and after the two-week settling down period.

Table 4. Conversation Before and After New Seating Arrangement.

	Brief interactions	Sustained interactions
Old arrangement	47	36
New arrangement	73	61

We see that both transitory and sustained interactions increased during the second period. There was also a remarkable increase in the amount of reading at this time. Before the study was begun, very few magazines were seen in the dayroom despite the fact that large quantities were purchased for the patients or donated each month. One reason for this was that there was no place to store magazines when they were not in use. If a magazine were to be placed on the floor, a nurse was likely to consider this untidy and remove it. The tables now provided places where printed materials could be left without fear of their immediate disappearance. Patients had formerly hoarded magazines, carrying them around in bundles or keeping them under mattresses where they would not be taken away. The same hoarding, which had been a sensible reaction considering the circumstances, appeared when we first laid out magazines on the tables. The first week we supplied 20 magazines a day but they disappeared as rapidly as we put them out. Later, when the ladies found that the magazines were brought to the ward regularly and could be left on the table safely, hoarding decreased.

At the same time the ward physician was so impressed with the transformation of the ward, that he sent an occupational therapist to the ward to develop a crafts program. He felt that craftwork could be done at the tables. None of our interaction recording was done during the crafts sessions, but there was an increase in craft activities throughout the day. Like magazine reading, this was a serendipitous outcome of the new ward arrangement, and has the further implication that it is difficult to keep change isolated and circumscribed. A hospital ward, like a commercial office or an army barracks, is a social system, and a change in any single element will change other parts too. When one introduces tables into a room, it is likely that the occupants will try to make the tables attractive and functional. Except under highly artificial and restricted laboratory situations, it is unlikely that environmental changes can involve only a single factor. If we study the effects of decreased noise in a commercial office, we might find that it produced lower absenteeism and fewer outside trips. One would thereby be recording interaction among more inhabitants than were present in the office before the change. Initial change produces secondary changes, which then affect the initial change, and it is difficult to determine whether an observable effect resulted from the initial change, one of the secondary changes, or a combination of all.

I found this study in the old folks' ward to be instructive, not only from the standpoint of improved institutional architecture, but also for the possibilities it presented of undertaking environmental research. It is standard procedure in psychological research to take environment for granted, or to consider it as a background against which interaction takes place. This study convinced me of the potentialities of behavioral research in which the total environment could be altered systematically according to an experimental plan. The pitfalls of undertaking this research using a single variable laboratory model were also apparent. Yet experimentation is only one of the methods used in the behavioral fields, and it is generally supplemented by interviews, natural observation, and questionnaire methods. In the next section we will describe the way that some of the other methods were used, not only on this particular old folks' ward, but in other hospital settings.

SOLICITING OPINIONS

Sometimes while listening to designers discussing the needs of office workers, students in dormitories, or mental patients, one can learn more about the speaker's own needs than about the needs of his customers. One reason for this is the social distance between the architect and the people for whom he is designing. Slum dwellers, store clerks, and state hospital patients are likely to come from social backgrounds different from those of the architects and administrators who supply the design specifications. At the state hospital we studied in Saskatchewan only a small percentage of patients came from homes with indoor plumbing. We do not know how many patients slept in single rooms before they entered hospital, but the number was not great. One study showed that patients came from families with an average of six children, and one out of five patients came from families with between ten and 19 children. Single hospital rooms, in fact, have been found undesirable, not only among natives of developing nations in Africa for whom isolation means social ostracism or imminent death, but also among patients surveyed in New York City[5] and the Royal Victoria Hospital in Belfast.[6] The Belfast survey involved a carefully selected sample of 148 adults who had been in hospital between seven and 14 days who were all interviewed in their homes. Some of the patients were dissatisfied with the very large wards—which contained 20 or more beds—but only two patients in the entire sample desired single rooms, and even this was qualified by their expressed preference for glass-sided cubicles. The six patients who had been in single rooms during past admissions all volunteered remarks to illustrate that the rooms had caused depressing feelings of isolation.

Particularly in dealing with low-income and minority groups one

[5] J. D. Thompson, "Patients Like These Four-Bed Wards," *Modern Hospital* (December 1955), p. 84.

[6] N. Y. Dudgeon and T. W. Davidson, *Some Reactions of Patients to Their Stay in Hospital* (Belfast: Belfast Hospital Management Committee, 1965).

finds designs that are often in direct conflict with the needs of the individuals. We made a study of an older park in Sacramento which was frequented largely by older retired men as well as by alcoholics. In actuality the two groups—the old-timers and the alcoholics—remained physically separate and could easily be identified through their appearance and manner. The retired men dress cleanly, are clean shaven, play cards frequently, and stay predominantly on the north side of the park. The alcoholics are frequently unshaven, walk unevenly, dress sloppily, cluster around an available bottle, and remain on the south side of the park. The city managers and passersby do not distinguish between these two groups and view the entire park population with distaste. Several years ago the park was redesigned. According to the former chairman of the City Planning Commission, the goals of the new design were to (1) make the park more attractive, (2) to correct the failing water system, and (3) to open the park up for use by individuals other than elderly persons and transients. He elaborated on the last point by speaking of the need to relieve the "ominous crowd look" that resulted from the men gathering in one section of the park. The method chosen to relieve the unsightly congestion was dispersion, to be accomplished by permanently separating the facilities. Sixteen large elm trees which provided an abundance of shade were cut down, and movable wooden benches were replaced by permanent benches. Needless to say, the users of the park were not consulted about these changes since the goal was to rid the park of the present users or at least make them less visible to passersby. While the cutting down of the trees served to increase the discomfort of the men, it did not drive them from the park. For one thing, few of the men had any other place to go. Nor was the "crowd look" relieved. On the contrary, the congestion in the few areas of the park still shaded was greatly increased. Areas which were in the hot sun were now virtually deserted.

This is a rather minor horror story in the field of urban renewal in poverty areas. One can find numerous instances where the needs of the local occupants are not only ignored but are deliberately frustrated. Fortunately there seems to be an increasing awareness, on the part of designers, of the need to bring local residents into planning decisions. This will inevitably raise questions on how they should be involved and ways for obtaining user opinions in a valid way.

In addition to obtaining accurate background information on the people who occupy the building or area, a designer should understand their personal worlds. How does a visitor to the hospital view "Staff Only" washrooms, and how do the nurses feel about separate dining facilities for doctors and administrators? Sociologist William Deane resided on a mental ward for a week without his identity being known, an experiment that most social scientists fancy but few have attempted. He observed that the hospital looked very different from the inside: "This is in no sense a perceptual distortion. It is rather a condition of seeing things through a different set of eyes, which has the effect of making the familiar appear unfamiliar." [7] Keys jingling in the locks and the sound of doors banging down the corridor had a new significance, just as an elevator in which one had been trapped for 12 hours would look different afterwards. These are actual perceptual changes, a shift in the way things really look. There is ample evidence that perception of all kinds is affected by continued viewing, whch makes bright colors appear duller and unusual patterns less startling. It is important to take this sort of habituation into account in designing places where people will spend long periods of time. An office that is bright and cheerful to a visitor may irritate someone who has worked there for years; illumination that is too bright for people walking through a factory may be suitable for workers accustomed to the noise, grime, and rush of the production line.

In our mental hospital work we wanted to see if long- and short-stay patients shared the same views about their environment. We decided to ask the sorts of questions one might put to a hotel guest—questions about ventilation, lighting, temperature, furniture, noise, privacy, crowding, and so forth. We chose two hospital wards, each of which contained a mixture of short-stay, medium-stay, and long-stay patients. The short-stay category included patients who had been hospitalized under two years, the medium-stay patients had been there between two and ten years, and the long-stay patients had been hospitalized ten years or longer. We looked first at the total number of complaints patients made about the environment—instances of a patient's stating the dayroom was too warm, his bed was uncomfortable, there wasn't enough privacy, and the like. Our results showed that long-stay patients made fewer complaints than medium- or short-stay patients. It is instructive to review some of their answers to specific items, not so much because the results are of current interest since, it is to be hoped, the days of large isolated institutions have passed, but to show the kinds of information that can be obtained by asking people about their surroundings. If meaningful information can be secured from people who have extreme difficulty in communicating and relating to others, the results should be even more useful when one interviews factory workers, library patrons, and airline passengers.

Patients were satisfied with the size of the dayroom, ceiling height,

[7] William Deane, "The Reactions of a Non-Patient to a Stay on a Mental Hospital Ward," *Psychiatry*, XXIV (1961), 67.

and corridor length and width. Since these were all larger than the corresponding spaces in private homes, it appeared that scale per se was not a pressing concern. Patients were satisfied with the temperature and ventilation, although a substantial number wanted the windows opened more frequently. Long-stay patients preferred sleeping dormitories or had no expressed preferences, while short- and medium-stay patients wanted smaller bedrooms or single rooms. Less than 30 per cent of the patients in any category explicitly preferred single rooms, although it is not known how these figures would have changed if single rooms had been available. The dining hall was considered crowded by 21 per cent of the patients, the dayroom by 21 per cent, the corridor by 30 per cent, the dormitory by 42 per cent, and the ward as a whole by 41 per cent. In each case the short- and medium-stay patients were more sensitive to crowding than the long-stay patients. The long-stay patients were satisfied with the bed arrangements in the dormitory, but the short- and medium-stay patients felt the beds were too close together. Most of the patients were satisfied with the speed at which people walked through the hospital. Interestingly, short-stay patients concentrated their complaints on people walking too slowly, whereas long-stay patients maintained that people walked too fast.

Each patient was asked if he had a place to go if he wanted to be away from other people. Half the patients answered affirmatively, and there was a slight trend for more long-stay patients to have private places of their own, which is in line with the idea that long-stay patients "nest." There was a striking difference between the two wards as to the location of the private places, largely due to the fact that one ward was locked most of the time, the other unlocked. On the locked ward the most common private places were the visiting room, toilet, veranda, and sitting room. On the unlocked ward, the most frequent single response was that the patient would go outside if she wanted to be alone. On the locked ward, not a single patient gave this response. The use of outside areas as habitable space is not always given sufficient attention in institutional architecture, perhaps because of the professional split between architecture and landscape architecture, or the administrative division between building management and grounds management. In residential colleges, tuberculosis sanitoria, Air Force bases, and think-factories, the best places to escape from people are out-of-doors. Landscaping the grounds to provide private places with durable furniture placed in shaded, wooded, or hedged areas deserves specific attention.[8] Often the grounds are landscaped

[8] Robert Sommer, "Going Outdoors for Study Space," *Landscape Architecture,* LVIII, No. 3 (1968), 196–98.

to provide an impressive vista for visitors or state legislators as they approach the buildings, with little provision for the residents to have private areas. Schizophrenic patients are usually able to scavenge the materials, nails, and tools to construct shanties and shacks for their private use when they have the opportunity. This practice is generally tolerated until the hospital administration becomes concerned about the appearance of the grounds and decrees the shacks must be removed.

Another excellent method for learning how other people view the world is to read autobiographies. It is surprising how many first-person accounts are available on almost any conceivable topic. One can find books by airplane pilots, coal miners, West Point graduates, prisoners of war, and circus performers in many languages and covering different periods in time. I have read more than 50 published autobiographies of mental patients, and I limited my selection to actual first-person accounts of hospitalized patients, excluding all fiction or accounts by disturbed people who were never hospitalized. Later I discovered two distinguished men, Dr. Walter Alvarez and the late professor Carney Landis, who had spent lifetimes collecting these books. Professor Landis possessed first-person accounts by mental patients going back to the fourteenth century. I found these books invaluable for understanding the ways in which being hospitalized affected a person's *Weltanschauung*. Christmas and other holidays were times of loneliness and remorse. The admissions routine, which strips a patient of all personal belongings including his wedding ring (to protect his valuables) and his clothing (to send them to the laundry to be marked) and requires him to answer questions asked by people who do not bother to introduce themselves, lies somewhere beween the tragic and the grotesque. Almost every case of visual hallucinations in these 50 autobiographies occurred under conditions of reduced visual stimulation, confirming the laboratory studies of sensory deprivation, in which people who are subjected to reduced sensory inputs are unable to focus their thoughts and frequently experience hallucinations.

Two points should be made clear in interpreting autobiographical material as well as interview responses. It is conceivable that a person writing an autobiography or answering a questionnaire is ignorant of the truth, tries to distort his answers, or deliberately tries to mislead others. We accept these possibilities and try to guard against them. I have always assumed that if a person is asked a reasonable question in a straightforward manner and has no reasons to conceal his opinions, either for self-aggrandizement or fear of the interviewer's reaction or society's ridicule or reprisal, he will answer honestly and to the best of his ability. What interests us is the way people see the world, and their opinions about themselves and their environments are valid data from this standpoint. If a person sees himself as unprejudiced and democractic but refuses to work or live alongside Negroes, his beliefs as well as his actions are relevant psychological facts. Indeed, if we wanted to change his actions we might take advantage of the seeming discrepancy between his actions and his values. When a man believes that his neighbors are unfriendly or hostile, it may be academic to inform him that there are more social clubs and parties per capita in his neighborhood than anywhere else in the city. Although a person's opinions may be "wrong" by some objective test, they still influence his behavior.

The second point to be considered is that opinion or even consensus does not necessarily provide the best yardstick for decision-making or policy formation. What a hospital patient wants is not necessarily what is best for him from society's standpoint. Society has certain objectives in building mental institutions, high schools, and public libraries although some users may not share these goals. It is probably easiest to document this with regard to mental patients and most difficult with regard to schools, especially when critics such as Paul Goodman and A. S. Neill have argued cogently for letting children do what they want. If a child chooses to play in the streets instead of learning Latin or mathematics, that is his prerogative. Neill assumes that a student will come to the material when he is ready, and if he reaches the age of 17 without a desire to learn geography, it is probable that he wouldn't have derived much benefit from enforced attendance in a geography class. But Summerhill is not a public institution built with society's goals in mind. It is a student-oriented school built with the child's individual growth as its *raison d'être* and in this sense differs from a mental hospital built with public funds to perform certain services for society. The twin goals most frequently associated with mental institutions are custody (removing unpleasant and unwanted people from society) and therapy (behavior change), and these goals may be in conflict with those the patient has set for himself. Knowing the schizophrenic's needs for isolation, it is possible to design mental institutions that make it easy for him to withdraw. Instead of long corridors and open dayrooms, we could provide many private areas, lockers and dressers where he could keep his belongings, and wooded areas where he could be secluded or build a shanty. A good architect can design for isolation and solitude just as creatively as he designs for custody and enforced behavior change. Most large mental institutions serve neither society's interests nor those of the patients. The security provisions are unnecessary except in a handful of cases where a different sort of institution, not a "mental hospital" is required. The best of today's mental institutions have done away with locked doors, fences and barricades, as well as constant surveillance by watchful attendants. From the standpoint of behavior change, mental institutions are even less effective. Most successful "cures" are simply a matter of the patient's remaining out of circulation while his objectionable behavior abates. It takes a while for a person to get over being angry or hurt or desperate, and custody sometimes provides the necessary respite. The question remains whether another type of environment without locked doors and personal indignities could accomplish this more effectively. There is no question that the shelters mental patients would design for themselves differ markedly from what society has provided or is likely to provide in the future to meet its own needs. It is possible to construct and design a Summerhill for mental patients, the sort of place where their anxieties are allayed through a minimization of social contacts. Determining whether patients would be rehabilitated into society from such institutions is as relevant as asking whether students will learn Latin at Summerhill.

This cautionary note (that what a person wants may not serve society's demands) does not lessen the need for discovering the individual's needs. Knowing that someone desires to isolate himself provides important clues as to what will happen when he is placed in an institution. We have found that he will seek out areas where he can be alone, even if this means a broom closet, fire escape, or toilet stall. Though some architects have accomplished this feat inadvertently, it is possible to construct a building with no private areas deliberately. Hospital architects have designed wards without nurses' stations, placing the nurse behind a counter at the intersection of radial patient areas. The rationale is to reduce kaffeeklatsches among nurses who minister to pills and charts rather than patients, but the result is a ward that provides privacy for no one. Patients generally have no control over their space-time, and nurses aides and technicians have only slightly more in the sense that their work schedules are set by higher authorities and they have no private offices to which to retreat. The hallmark of the professional is that he has his own private space and can control his use of time.

Lipman sees some positive value in the sociofugal arrangements employed in old folks homes. He feels that they satisfy the patient's desire to withdraw and disengage himself from active social situations or at least reduce social relationships to a number that the patient finds manageable. Virtually all of the conversations in the old folks homes were limited to immediate seat neighbors and such conversations were terminated by means of readily understood signals such as nudging, folding one's arms, or closing one's eyes.[9] Sociofugal arrangements offer a person the opportunity to withdraw from social interaction when he wishes to do so without the necessity of physically removing himself from the presence of other people.

Asking people what they want in the way of an environment helps overcome institutional alienation and depersonalization. A second stage of client-customer interaction occurs when the reasons for the various design features are explained, particularly if the client's expressed needs cannot be met. The Roper and Gallup Organizations are built on the idea that people like to be asked for their opinions. Positive rapport is strongest, sometimes bordering on gratitude and obsequiousness, when the respondent believes his opinion will make a difference. Catherine Vavra, a public health nurse who surveyed patients in a tuberculosis sanitorium, reported these reactions: "This survey is the finest thing that has been done here," and "If you did more of this, we'd like it." [10] An occupational therapist asked the residents of a geriatrics ward about the best colors for knitting wools and expressed surprise at how grateful the ladies were to be asked for their opinions.[11] Surveys among underdogs are doubly important, since they are not only among the most numerous of consumers but also the ones most likely to feel powerless and alienated from decision-making. In the hospital survey reported previously we found that patients who had been in hospitals a long time were least likely to make complaints. This sort of docility is generally characteristic of long-stay inmates in any sort of institution. Anthony Heckstal-Smith, a prisoner himself, described a guard's concept of a model convict as "one who does his own time, never gives trouble, and always submits to authority." [12] The same passivity in the face of the environment is a major ingredient of what is called prisonitis, hospitalism, and institutional neurosis. We do not know whether the lack of complaints is due to feelings of resignation and powerlessness, the belief that complaints have no effect except that of bringing opprobrium to the inmate, or sensory blunting after prolonged incarceration. Katz found that short-stay mental patients preferred colors such as red and yellow from the short-wave end of the spectrum, whereas long-stay patients preferred the cooler

[9] Lipman, in press, *op. cit.*

[10] Catherine E. Vavra and E. D. Rainboth, "A Patients' Opinion Survey at Firland Sanitorium," *Public Health Reports*, LXXI (1956), 351–59.

[11] D. Susan Cross, "Color Preferences of Older Patients," *Canadian Journal of Occupational Therapy*, XXVII (1960), 9–12.

[12] Anthony Heckstal-Smith, *Eighteen Months* (London: Allen Wingate, 1954), p. 32.

blues and greens at the other end of the spectrum.[13] The tepid and drab institutional environment undoubtedly has some role in the shock inmates suffer when going outside for the first time. Convicts frequently report becoming dizzy or ill when first leaving prison. Peter Wildeblood, upon release from prison where he served a one-year sentence, wrote, "The world was strange and a little frightening; the traffic roared and pounced, the colors of women's dresses, flowers and neon signs, jabbed the nerves of my eyes and music had a rich new texture as tangible as fur or silk." [14] Another ex-convict described his first reaction to San Francisco:

> The noise of streetcars and vehicles bothered me, but I tried to see every-thing. The scurrying people going in all directions seemed strange. Never before, even though I had been raised in and near a great me-tropolis, had I realized so keenly what a rush life is. . . . The noises on Market Street distressed me, and besides, my eyes pained. They were so unused to seeing rapidly moving vehicles and so many strange faces.[15]

An English convict wrote, "My first impression was that everything was speeded up. When I got on a bus at Parkhurst, the speed of it whizzing along the country roads sickened me." [16] The only time the slow tempo of life in a mental hospital changes is 5:00 p.m. when the nurses' shift ends. The scuffling walk characteristic of long-stay patients who have been crowded together too long has become even more pro-nounced than it used to be through heavy doses of tranquilizers.

Surveys he conducted in 17 British old folks homes led Lipman to question the assumption made by the Ministry of Health that social life in geriatric homes centered about the patients' bedrooms. He found that virtually all of the social life in the homes took place in the sitting room and to a lesser extent in the dining area. Although patients knew where others typically sat in the dayroom, they did not know where others slept. Except in cases of prolonged illness, visiting in bedrooms simply did not occur.[17] As we shall see in Chapter 9, the reverse situation obtains in college dormitories where the lounges are

[13] S. E. Katz, "Color Preferences in the Insane," *Journal of Abnormal and Social Psychology,* XXVI (1931), 203–9.

[14] Peter Wildeblood, *Against the Law* (New York: Julian Messner Publications, 1959), p. 172.

[15] Donald Lowrie, *My Life Out of Prison* (New York: Mitchell Kennerly Publisher, 1915), p. 39.

[16] Wilfred Macartney, *Walls Have Mouths* (London: Victor Gollancz Ltd., 1936), p. 432.

[17] Lipman, 1968, *op. cit.*

used infrequently and most of the student's time in the dormitory is spent in his own room. An explanation for this difference is the greater mobility of the students to move from room to room in contrast to the elderly patients who are often infirm and inactive. Knowledge about the social life of the residents must clearly be taken into account in the design of social areas.

A mild dissent to the use of surveys is made by architect Raymond Studer who is influenced by the behaviorist B. F. Skinner. Advocating instead the direct observation of behavior, Studer feels that verbal statement from people as to "what they want" or "what they need" are, at most, of indirect relevance since these reports are shaped by random and irrelevant events, including interview bias and linguistic difficulties, as well as a person's lack of experience in different sorts of environments.[18] There would, indeed, be little point in asking most Americans how they would feel about living in round structures, if one's goal were to secure informed opinion. On the other hand, there is no harm in asking the question, even as matters now stand, as long as the replies are considered in the light of the respondent's inexperience. Another objection to the use of surveys is the frequent practice of making them substitutes for remedial action. A city council that formerly referred an unpopular proposal to committee now undertakes a survey. Though I would defend the proposition that surveys are inherently humanizing, they become dishonest when they are undertaken without a spirit of open inquiry. The hospital survey described previously had many implications, both for remedial action in the particular hospital and for the design of similar institutions not yet built. The obvious remedy to the complaints about crowding would involve building additional wards, which would solve the immediate problem but would also make a large unwieldy institution even larger and less efficient. A better remedy is to discharge patients who do not need to be inside the hospital, which was, in fact, the practice followed.[19]

The lack of private places on locked wards can be remedied by increasing the size of the ward or by creating more differentiated spaces, but a more reasonable solution is to unlock the doors and permit the patients to find private areas on the grounds. Knowing the basis of a problem does not reduce the need for creative thought to find the most effective solution. In this particular instance the changes were

[18] Raymond G. Studer, "On Environmental Programming," *Arena* (May 1966), 290–96.

[19] This institution, which had 1500 patients in 1961, was down to 600 patients in 1968. The Superintendent may have the signal honor of becoming the first mental hospital superintendent to work himself out of a job.

undertaken with knowledge of the patients' viewpoints as well as the sorts of things that bothered the nurses, physicians, and state legislators. The end result, which was to reduce the number of patients confined in the institution, seems to benefit everyone's interest even though, at the outset, some nurses were afraid their jobs might be abolished, some patients were troubled by the prospects of living outside, and state legislators were apprehensive about the costs of extensive boarding programs.

In this chapter we have seen the effects of environmental programming (or the lack of it) within a mental hospital, a setting well suited to such observation. Of course, one must be aware of the differences between a setting that totally encompasses the individual's life and one in which he is a casual visitor. Yet there is much to be learned from places where society keeps its rejects. Psychiatrist David Vail has said that:

> The mental institution holds a mirror to life. If we can learn how evil is done in that microcosm, we may learn how evil is done in the world around. And if we learn how, we may then learn why. More importantly if we learn how evil is done to the human spirit, we may learn someday how it can be undone.[20]

Suitable architecture is especially necessary in places like mental hospitals where the patients are extraordinarily passive and dependent. For the most part, they are not going to arrange their rooms to suit their needs; it is up to others to do it. The task cannot be left to custodians and those more concerned with neatness and ease of maintenance than with therapy.

[20] David Vail, *Dehumanization and the Institutional Career* (Springfield, Ill.: Charles C Thomas, Publisher, 1966).

7

Designed for Learning

It is curious that such suggestions (paying high salaries to teachers, treating students as individuals, and grouping them according to their abilities) rarely deal with the actual processes of teaching or learning. They make no attempt to analyse what is happening when a student listens to a lecture, reads a book, writes a paper, or solves a problem. (B. F. Skinner, *Teaching Machines*)

CLASSROOM SPACES

Interior classroom space is all too frequently taken for granted by those who plan educational facilities as well as those who use them. Designers lack adequate criteria of classroom efficiency; teachers and students tend to adopt a fatalistic attitude toward school buildings. There is agreement from all parties that a school's physical plant should mirror its educational philosophy, but the methods for achieving isomorphism are elusive. The present rectangular room with its straight rows of chairs and wide windows was intended to provide for ventilation, light, quick departure, ease of surveillance, and a host of other legitimate needs as they existed in the early 1900's. Before the advent of the electric light, it often required legislative action to compel economy-minded school boards to provide adequate fenestration. The typical long narrow shape resulted from a desire to get light across the room. The front of each room was determined by window location, since pupils had to be seated so that window light came over the left shoulder. Despite new developments in lighting, acoustics, and structures, most schools are still boxes filled with cubes each containing a specified number of chairs in straight rows. There have been attempts to break away from this rigid pattern, but experimental schools are the exception rather than the rule.

The American classroom is dominated by what has been called the rule of two-thirds—two-thirds of the time someone is talking and two-thirds of this time it is the teacher, and two-thirds of the time that the teacher is talking, she is lecturing, giving directions or criticizing behavior. Movement in and out of classrooms and the school building itself is rigidly controlled. Everywhere one looks there are "lines"— generally straight lines that bend around corners before entering the auditorium, the cafeteria, or the shop. The linear pattern of parallel rows reinforces the lines. The straight rows tell the student to look ahead and ignore everyone except the teacher, the students are jammed so tightly together that psychological escape, much less physical separation, is impossible. The teacher has 50 times more free space than the students with the mobility to move about. He writes important messages on the blackboard with his back to his students. The august figure can rise and walk among the lowly who lack the authority even to stand without explicit permission. Teacher and children may share the same classroom but they see it differently. From a student's eye level, the world is cluttered, disorganized, full of people's shoulders, heads, and body movements. His world at ground level is colder than the teacher's world. She looms over the scene like a helicopter swooping down to ridicule or punish any wrongdoer. Like Gulliver in Lilliput the teacher has a clear view of what is going on. She sees order and organization and any deviation from it. The child is expected to

> sit on a hard seat, not to move, scrape his feet, or gaze out the window . . . to listen, to answer questions by raising his hand, to draw neat lines in a book and write or script-print on a single blue line in exactly the same way as all his peers. He may be permitted to ask questions but, for the most part he is expected to conform. The teacher teaches, the child listens. He soon appreciates the advantages of conformity.[1]

Maria Montessori likened the children in such schools to "butterflies mounted on pins, fastened each to his desk, spreading the useless wings of barren and meaningless knowledge they have acquired." [2]

Spatial restrictions are paralleled by administrative rules that are im-

---

[1] O. A. Oeser, *Teacher, Pupil, and Task* (London: Tavistock Publications, 1955), p. 37.

[2] M. Montessori, *Spontaneous Activity in Education* (Cambridge, Mass.: Robert Bentley, Inc., 1964).

posed from above and that the child has no voice in shaping. New programs, teachers, and activities come and go without explanation. On the positive side, this may be good training for an adult world of deadlines, rush hours, crowding, impersonality, and alienation from work. The child begins I.T.A. reading and next year finds himself in a class of Programmed Readers. As he grows older, he moves into cubicles with larger chairs and taller students. Even high schools provide few places for students to linger, so they congregate in the corridors, outside the locker rooms, or in the stairwells seeking refuge from crowd pressures and impersonal authority. Intimacy is discouraged and students cannot hold hands in the corridors. A student learns his place in society and what others expect of him from the way that teachers and administrators conduct the social system of the school. He acquires attitudes that derogate self-respect and create the self-image of a pitiful figure at a standard desk whose physical presence is required by statute. These aspects of educational life are derived more from classroom form than from the new math or computer logic. Here is Edgar Friedenberg's description of Milgrim High:

> There is no physical freedom whatsoever at Milgrim. . . . No time at which, or place in which, a student may simply go about his business. Privacy is strictly forbidden. Except during class breaks, the toilets are kept locked, so that a student must not only obtain a pass but find the custodian and induce him to unlock the facility.[3]

The range diversity of furniture available for classroom use is surprising. One has to leaf through the catalogues of major furniture manufacturers to observe the countless styles of tables, desks, and chairs. Furniture manufacturers bear little direct responsibility for uncomfortable and unsuitable classroom furniture, except that they make it available to people who want it and they make little attempt to evaluate the furniture in use, apart from anthropometric studies of body dimensions. One cannot blame a manufacturer who advertises that his lecture room furniture is "permanently attached to the floor on pedestals or risers to keep the room neat and easy to maintain." No school board is required to purchase such chairs, but the school board lacks reliable information on how particular items work in practice. The best they can do is visit other schools to see what is being used. The manufacturer looking for a wide market for his product has a stake in behavioral data, although he may feel that such research is uneconomic considering the total market. Research into educational facilities can

[3] Edgar Z. Friedenberg, *Coming of Age in America* (New York: Random House, Inc., 1963), p. 29.

also originate in schools of education or design, which would also have the advantage of being independent of pressures to endorse specific products. Thus far, the interface between education and design has remained relatively unexplored—educators being mainly concerned with student behavior and designers with aspects of the physical environment.

Obsolete facilities or shortages of classroom space can produce innovations in teaching methods and classroom organization. There are many instances of classes being held in gymnasia, corridors, school libraries, and the school auditorium. Unfortunately there has been little systematic evaluation of these natural experiments. Coping with a bad environment is a common element in the existential situation of students and teachers intersecting in space-time. It would be profitable for a teacher to spend at least a fraction of one class period discussing ways to make the environment more tolerable for all concerned. This would also help tune in the students to the lighting, ventilation, noise level, and arrangement of desks as functional and changeable aspects of environment. I recall my first semester of high school geometry when, because of an acute shortage of classrooms, we met in the chemistry lab and sat on benches around the walls of the room. I was a "C" student simply because I could not see the blackboard and was too self-conscious to walk into the center of the room and peer at the blackboard. When we moved into a conventional classroom at midyear and my poor eyes earned me a front seat, my grades improved markedly. I have often wondered how many children are doing poorly in school because of bad lighting, acoustics, or being too cold or warm, and are unable, because of shyness or lack of opportunity, to explain their predicament to the teacher.

Not every educator accepts present room furnishings as necessary and desirable. The Bureau of Laboratory Schools at the University of Texas has experimented with "work center classroom furniture," which contains a variety of items that can be used for different but simultaneous activities with only half as many individual desks as there are pupils in the room. The rationale is that individual desks are needed only for certain types of activities. For a class of 32 children the following furniture was provided:

Two rectangular tables, six feet in length.
Two round tables, three-and-one-half feet in diameter.
Eight table-desks, three feet square. These were essentially two desks joined back to back. Four book compartments were placed on each of these desks, enough for the 32 pupils.
Thirty-two pupil chairs.

Stuffed upholstered furniture consisting of two pupil chairs and a settee
    large enough to accommodate two children.
Two movable bookcases four feet long, mounted on rubber casters.
Two easels.
A teacher's chair and desk.

All pieces were fully portable and could be moved easily and quickly.
They provided each student with an individual book compartment
and storage area but not an individual or permanently assigned work
surface.[4] When the "work center" arrangement was evaluated by
Sanders, he found that the movable chairs rarely moved in practice.
He lamented the seeming unawareness among teachers and administrators of the importance of room arrangements. It required only 1.4
minutes to make a major rearrangement of the work center furniture
(more than 75 per cent of the pieces) and a smaller move took less
than a minute, yet for the most part the furniture remained stationary.
Without teacher education and in-service training to increase environmental sensitivity, he doubted the value of innovations in classroom
layout.[5]

What we see in the schoolroom today are few attempts to adapt to
new educational philosophy and technology, but more or less straightforward attempts to deal with increasing enrollment by building more
of the same. The basic classroom was intended to serve a "sit and
learn" educational program in which teachers did most of the talking
and the pupils read assigned sections or answered questions orally or
in writing. Criticism made nearly a generation ago of this form seems
apt today:

If the recitation and reproduction of lessons is considered the chief
aim of teaching, the traditional equpment of the classroom is perhaps
sufficient. But if teaching is guiding children to do their own thinking,
purposing, planning, executing, and appraising, as recent educational
philosophy maintains, then the classroom becomes a workshop, a library,
a museum, in short, a learning laboratory.[6]

Howard Rolfe also believed traditional classrooms with fixed row
seating to be unsuitable for group discussions, pupil interaction, and
a variety of activities taking place simultaneously. When he compared,

[4] Henry J. Otto, "An Experiment with Elementary School Classroom Seating and
Equipment," *Texas School Board Journal*, II (December 1955), 3–6.
[5] D. C. Sanders, *Innovations in Elementary School Classroom Seating*, Bureau of
Laboratory Schools Publication No. 10. (Austin: University of Texas, 1958).
[6] C. E. Lewis, "Equipping the Classroom as a Learning and Teaching Laboratory,"
The American Schoolboard Journal, CL (1940), 29.

within the same school district, activities in traditional classrooms with those in new, larger classrooms with portable furniture, he was quite discouraged by the sameness. Whether a teacher had ample room or little room, fixed or movable chairs, ample or limited storage space, made little difference in individual class activities, teaching methods, or the range of activities.

> The major conclusion is that the increase of 18 to 30 per cent of storage-free area in the large classroom over the small classroom, merely had the effect of pushing out the walls to make the perimeter area of the rooms wider, thereby enlarging these areas for instructional purposes and making the classrooms less confining and more comfortable. . . . They did little, however, to change the pattern of teaching or to change traditional use of classroom space for instruction. Space use and learning situations were, in large measure, determined by a pattern of teaching that except for a few deviations was the same in both small and large classrooms: a pattern of teaching that persisted regardless of differences in classroom size, features, equipment, or design.[7]

It can be added that the teachers themselves believed that class environment made a difference. A large majority in the small classrooms complained that their rooms were too crowded, noisy, cramped, inflexible, and unsuited for a variety of activities. According to Rolfe, all of the teachers in the large classrooms expressed satisfaction at room size, and the majority expressed enthusiasm for the total classroom environment. In their opinion, the large rooms with portable chairs made teaching easier and gave them a feeling they could do more.

> They appreciated their classrooms as comfortable, inspirational places to teach. Their classrooms made them feel there was no limit to what they could do if they desired. They said there was space for large and small group work, for dancing, and for project work. Pupils' desks were easy to move to clear space for activities and for group work. *They were quick to emphasize, however, that the large classroom had not changed their teaching methods.*[8]

It is clear that instructors must learn how to use available space and facilities. Just as one cannot provide a tractor for villagers in Thailand without showing them how to use it, one cannot introduce innovations in teaching environments without discussing new program possibilities with the instructional staff, pupils, and parents. Otherwise

[7] Howard C. Rolfe, "Observable Differences in Space Use of Learning Situations in Small and Large Classrooms," (Ph.D. thesis, University of California at Berkeley, 1961), p. 279.

[8] *Ibid.*, p. 192. Italics mine.

it is likely that people will do what they have done before even though a greater range of action is possible. Possibly they will do it less well because the new environment is designed for other sorts of activities. Fixed seating made the janitors' lives easy, but was introduced to provide a different sort of educational milieu. If the school traditions make the straight-row arrangement immutable, even though the chairs are portable, portable chairs serve only to increase the workload of the janitors who have to straighten the rows every evening.

The most radical departures from straight-row layout are found in schools utilizing open plan architecture for team teaching. In these "schools without walls" several grades share a large open space.[9] An increase in interaction between teacher and pupil and between teacher and teacher and the possibility of shifting children into performance groups in particular subjects are the major goals of the new arrangements. Eliminating the cubicles permits teachers to see how others work. Except under very unusual circumstances, a teacher has no occasion to visit another classroom once his days of practice teaching are finished. The students have the opportunity to observe and identify with several adult figures rather than a single teacher during the entire school day.

When I visited a cooperative school conducted along these lines, I complimented the teacher on the spatial freedom allowed the students. Some students were sitting on their chairs and leaning forward on their tables in rapt attention, but a few were at the periphery of the room looking out the window or working on their own projects. The head teacher accepted my comments graciously, but added ruefully that many parents objected to "the kids not paying attention." He wondered how often pupils in traditional straight-row classrooms lost attention in the proceedings. This seemed an apt consideration, since these signs of gross inattention—the students sitting away from the group working on their own projects—are more evident where there is spatial freedom. When the pupils are seated in straight rows facing ahead, the casual observer has the illusion that virtually everyone is attending to what is going on in the front of the room.

Some of the newer English schools have been more receptive than their American counterparts to open plan arrangements. A visitor to several new British schools commented:

> The physical layout of the classrooms is markedly different from ours. American teachers are coming to appreciate the importance of a flexible room. However, even in good elementary schools, this usually means

[9] Educational Facilities Laboratories, *Schools Without Walls* (New York: Educational Facilities Laboratories, 1965).

having movable, rather than fixed desks. In these [English] classes there
are no individual desks and no assigned places. Around the room which
is about the size of one of ours, there are different tables for different
kinds of activities: art, water, sand play, and numbers work. The numbers tables have all kinds of number lines—strips of paper with numbers
marked on them in sequence on which children learn to count and reason automatically—beads, buttons, and odd things to count; weights and
balances; dry and liquid measures, and a rich variety of apparatus for
learning basic mathematical concepts.[10]

Freedom from time restrictions in these schools parallels the spatial
freedom. The teacher develops the day's routine as he chooses and he
generally leaves many options to the children. Spatial freedom will not
insure educational innovation. Presented to an unsure and inadequate
teacher, it will result in greater efforts at discipline in order to keep
people together and "on the same track" once the fixed rows of chairs,
which greatly aided in discipline, are eliminated. The spatial freedom
will only help those teachers already committed to individual or small
group instructions or willing to try it. Temporal, spatial, and administrative freedom go hand in hand. Temporal freedom is not very useful
if one is shut in a rigid box with prescribed activities. Spatial freedom
is undermined when a teacher has to operate at a tight schedule and
perform activities that require rigid spatial arrangements. Administrative freedom is undermined by tight little cubicles and unchange-
able 50-minute hours. Ideally all three occur together but if I as a
teacher could have only one of the three, I would choose administrative
freedom—the support and encouragement from my superiors to inno-
vate and develop a program suited to the needs of my students. Given
support and encouragement from above, I could accommodate myself at
some slight cost in time and energy to an unsuitable space-time world.

Spatial innovations often flow naturally from program innovations.
At Rochdale College, a counter-institution that grew out of Toronto's
cooperative student housing movement and that awards no degrees,
gives no examinations, and has no entrance requirements or criteria
for leaving, one of the two salaried "resource people" describes his
reactions during the planning of a new building for the college.

When the college started moving into its space, the first thing Ian
MacKenzie and I did was to plan for our offices. This seemed eminently
reasonable and we were close to having the renovations done when one
of the students asked why we needed offices in the first place. I don't
think Ian or I took the question seriously at first . . . After a bit,
though, we realized that he was perfectly right. Why should two members

[10] J. Featherstone, "What's Happening in British Classrooms," *New Republic*
(August 26, 1967), p. 18.

of the college have offices to themselves when we were crying for space? And, more important, wouldn't that institutionalize everything we were trying to get beyond—both in other people's responses and in ourselves. Certainly it would. We would set up office hours, we would come and do office work, we would start playing all sorts of roles, not because we felt right playing those roles but because the bloody offices demanded them of us. We canned the idea and instead we installed a number of desks, with a typewriter and phone, which anyone can come and use (including us) for reading, writing, or office work.[11]

Technical innovations in the area of information systems will affect school design. According to MacConnell, it will soon be possible to arrange eight different television monitors around a table to enable students to view different programs on each monitor, all without wires. The communications system will be based on laser beams conveyed through carpeting or other floor surfaces.[12] Teaching machines, talking typewriters, and computerized information storage-retrieval systems will affect school design, probably first in the library and audio-visual aids departments, and eventually in the classroom itself. Unified schools, which replaced individual frame schoolhouses, are being combined into educational parks containing a variety of specialized functions. A combination of the population explosion, educational television, programmed instruction, and the shorter work week may return some classroom functions to the home and to parents. The movement of large amounts of capital into service fields, already evident in the construction of reitrement centers, low rental housing, and college dormitories, may find its way into school construction. There is no reason why private firms cannot construct classrooms to be rented to school districts on a long- or short-term basis. In college housing, private builders often provide more attractive and comfortable housing with superior amenities for less money than the cumbersome state bureaucracy. It is an axiom on most university campuses that a light bulb purchased from the university warehouse costs twice as much as the same light bulb purchased downtown with petty cash. Private classrooms were widely used during the Middle Ages. Each master contracted for space on an individual basis, which led to considerable competition for the best rooms. In several places the competition became so fierce that a code of ethics was developed. The University of Paris code promulgated in 1244 decreed that no master could retain more than one classroom or bid a higher price for a room already

---

[11] Dennis Lee, "Getting to Rochdale," *This Magazine Is About Schools*, II (Winter 1968), 86.

[12] J. D. MacConnell, "Planning the School Environment," (Paper presented at the Second National Conference on Architectural Psychology, Park City, Utah, 1966).

rented by another man. Disputes between masters were settled through recourse to higher authority. Boniface of Genoa wrote to the Count and Duchess of Milan in 1403 to protest the illegal occupancy by Master Bertoloneus of quarters that rightfully belonged to the more experienced and senior Master Luchino. The Rector made a strong case for Luchino, "a most excellent doctor of long standing," compared to the inexperienced Bertoloneus whose students "rarely attended classes." [13]

Substantial revenue could be realized from the sale of air rights over schools in the heart of the city. Three stories in a high school could be used for academic purposes, and the space above for offices, with separate entrances for each. This kind of merger would help reduce the institutional isolation of schools and pupils, but at the same time, there would be no more confusion between school and office activities than if the school were located around the corner from the office building. Several housing projects have placed schools at the ground floor in residential buildings. Advantages of joint occupancy include economy, elimination of dangerous crossings, improved community spirit, and greater utilization of school space for community purposes in the evenings and summers.[14]

Blurring of the division between public and private responsibility in the area of university construction is now taking place. The rental of classroom space already occurs with modulux units—temporary structures leased for specified periods with a purchase option thereafter. On campuses across the country it has been easier to finance the rental of these temporary structures than to float bond issues for permanent buildings. One noted east coast university has mortgaged its academic buildings to finance residence hall construction. Some fraternity houses are privately owned but built on college land, whereas others are college-owned and rented to fraternities for designated periods. At Florida Atlantic University, the first American institution designed solely for upper division and graduate study, the University provides offices that are rented to students on a semester basis. Some colleges provide parking facilities for all students and faculty at no charge. Others rent spaces on campus, and still others expect public transportation and private garages to serve the campus. There seems no necessary reason why a school at any level must own a physical plant. File cabinets, dictaphones, typewriters, desks, and chairs can also be rented on a yearly or long-term basis.

[13] Lynn Thorndike, *University Records and Life in the Middle Ages* (New York: Columbia University Press, 1944).

[14] Jonathan King, "In Which the Bell Tolls," Saturday Review (September 17, 1960), p. 99.

The technical means for gaining increased flexibility in school design, albeit at increased cost, have raised questions about the proportion of the building to be committed to convertible space such as a cafetorium or library–study hall. There are many architects and administrators who feel that flexibility is desirable, but sometimes its cost is too great. Not only can the sense of transience and impermanence adversely affect morale, but the residents may not know how to allocate space efficiently and the results will be spatial confusion and discord. Walter Netsch, who designed the Chicago campus of the University of Illinois, shunned large scale convertibility and provided instead a diversity of spaces. One drawback of flexibility is that it precludes the use of specific design features intended to optimize particular functions. The architect who tries to serve all masters may serve none well. The high school auditorium that must serve as a gymnasium, dance hall, and theater is likely to fail in all capacities. There is a point at which the price of flexibility is too high in terms of functional efficiency. Since teaching methods are changing, and it is difficult to forecast where things are going, the best alternative to infinite flexibility and "loose-fitting space" is to provide for many different sorts of spaces so that a new activity can be accommodated somewhere within the existing structure. No one is able to state with any certainty how programmed instruction, computer aids, and subprofessional teacher assistants will affect the organizational structure and building needs of future schools. Architects do not like designing structures that are obsolete before completion, an unusually idealistic position in a society built on planned obsolescence. My own experience has been that architects are genuinely interested in planning buildings for changing functions that require flexible spaces as well as a diversity of spaces. If two rooms are intended to serve the same function, it is desirable to make them slightly different unless the cost is prohibitive. One conference room can be long and narrow, the other short and squat. One lecture room can have a podium in front of the blackboard and the other can do without it. This provides the user with greater flexibility in assigning spaces. The necessary concomitant is that space assignment policies must take into account the variety of spaces available. The random assignment of individuals to exotic and unusual spaces will result in greater dissatisfaction than assigning everyone to traditional all-purpose spaces. Our discussion is as relevant to space assignment and utilization as it is to the design process.

The fuzzy thinking about behavioral aspects of school design is well illustrated by discussions of windowless schools. The arguments on both sides are the same ones greeting any change. At first the opponents argue against its technical feasibility—you cannot properly light or ventilate windowless rooms, fire protection will be inadequate, and so forth. As the technical solutions to these objections are developed, the opponents take recourse in psychological and social needs—windowless schools are unnatural, daylight has an inherent advantage over artificial light, claustrophobia will result from fully enclosed spaces, and so on. If it were merely a matter of weighing the technical advantages of windowless schools—minimizing dust, outside noises, and distractions, and providing full temperature and light control—against the "soft" social-psychological variables, there is no question but that windowless schools would carry the day. However, the course of the argument has been affected by the existence of social scientists whose job it is to harden the soft data. If it can be proved that learning is poor or students begin to hallucinate in the monotonous environment, one is able to trump the ace of the technocrats by arguing that the technically feasible windowless solution is not functional in terms of society's requirement that the students emerge from school at the end of the day, if not educated, at least undamaged. At present the pro-window forces still lack behavioral data in support of their case and argue on the basis of metaphor and supposition, but their arguments must be weighed against statistics such as those from the windowless school in New Mexico that is reported to have 40 per cent greater efficiency in heating and cooling, constant lighting to prevent eye-strain, partitions, doors, and walls with a 35 decibel or more noise reduction, and reduced maintenance costs.[15] The controversy about windowless classrooms seems trivial with the advent of the under-ground school. The Abo School was built entirely underground with a Federal subsidy and can double as an air-raid shelter in the event of an emergency. Interestingly it was built in a county that already had windowless schools and whose officials were firm believers in a con-trolled teaching climate. Advantages of the plan include the availa-bility of all four walls for teacher use. In some rooms the chairs are arranged diagonally so pupils can see two walls without discomfort. The only behavioral data of any reliability that has emerged from the controversy is that claustrophobic reactions in the clinical sense are exceedingly rare. It is possible that claustrophobia-prone students and teachers transfer to other schools and districts (although there is no evidence for this), but the lack of such reactions is important be-havioral data. Opponents now take recourse in the need for com-munion with nature, contact with the outside, and stimulus variation, which are more difficult to measure and whose importance is not

[15] R. A. Frye and Frank Standhardt, "See More, Hear More, Learn More in Win-dowless Rooms," *Educational Screen and Audio-Visual Guide,* XL (June 1961), 227.

readily apparent. Should one show that communion with nature is reduced in windowless schools, is there "evidence" that this is harmful to students? Just to make my position clear, there is also no evidence that it does the student any good or does not harm him in some way. Behavioral work dealing with complex human needs must be a two-stage affair, first demonstrating that a need exists, and second relating its satisfaction or frustration to some criterion. In most cases the second step is the more difficult since criteria of human well-being are matters of some controversy. For instance, one can show that a democratic student-oriented teacher can elicit more class discussion than an authoritarian teacher, but whether class discussion is desirable or undesirable depends on its relation to other criteria such as the amount of material learned, the type of society in which the students live, and the content of the discussion. It is laudable to make man the measure of buildings, but there is no agreement about which man should be the yardstick.

Let us examine an experiment in which features of classroom environment were related to student behavior, an experiment that arose out of my own needs as a teacher. All too frequently I found myself assigned to classrooms that were unsuitable for my purposes. Some had a wide gap between my desk and the students, a no-man's-land which I tried to bridge by moving nearer the students and separating myself irrevocably from the blackboard or moving the students' chairs a few feet ahead if I arrived early enough to move the desks. In smaller rooms I experimented with semicircular arrangements and moved the class outside on the lawn as frequently as possible. In one seminar we met in a different room each period. I think we learned more from our travels than from class presentations. I have also been asked to assist other teachers with their space problems. Before giving advice, I always visit the class to see what is happening. It is surprising how much one can learn from observing where students sit—are the fearful huddled in the rear with the front rows empty, or in isolated bands searching for their lost leader, or is there a cohesive and intensive focus to the seating? Many teachers are blind to the physical distribution of the students so long as attendance can be taken, discipline is maintained, cheating is minimized, and boys and girls are not holding hands publicly. A teacher may sense that something is wrong, he is not getting through to his students, participation is poor, and the class hour is mutually frustrating, but he does not know whether this is due to the students, their parents, the course content, his method of presentation, the time of day, or what. The distribution of students within the room represents an accommodation to their environment that goes on to influence subsequent behavior. It is unlikely that we can find a simple causal chain: dull teacher drives students to the rear, which results in low participation. Each factor relates to the others in very complex ways. Low participation leads the teacher to conclude that students are disinterested, which lowers his own motivation still further. Students conclude from the lack of participation that none is desired and maintain their silence. Since all this complexity stands as an inexplicit and conceptually cloudy background to the teacher-student relationship, appropriate remedies will be difficult to specify.

CLASSROOM LAYOUT AND STUDENT PARTICIPATION

My curiosity about classroom seating had been whetted by teachers' assumptions about students' seating: the front rows contain the most interested students, those in the rear engage in illicit activities, students at the aisles are mainly concerned with quick departures, most absentees come from the rear quadrant most distant from the windows, and the straight-row arrangement inhibits discussion. Fact or fiction? Any teacher could supply a dozen concordant or discordant examples at will. The anecdotes seem to agree on the fact that classroom space can be divided into zones containing people who behave differently,[16] but whether zones are selected by those people in the first place or affect them afterwards, or some combination of the two, remained unclear. If shoulder-to-shoulder seating discouraged conversation in old folks' home, what did it do to a student's attitude toward school and the teacher's attitude toward the students? Does it make a student feel like raw material in an educational assembly line, something to be shaped, worked on, and processed? Is it degrading to sit shoulder to shoulder with strangers front and back, to be so close together to people alongside that knees touch, where privacy is impossible, and one cannot adjust his trousers without making a public display? I tend to forget what it is like until those occasions when I have to attend lectures held in classrooms. Without exception I have been appalled by the closeness of the seats. Frequently the chairs are locked together and cannot be separated without the organized cooperation of everyone in the row. The next person's notebook is practically in front of my eyes. I am not used to focusing my attention on such a narrow field. My office desk is four times the size of a student's writing surface,

---

[16] As was mentioned in Chapter 6, nurses on mental wards do this also. The spatial categorization of people seems to be a fact of institutional life.

and papers on the right or left side of my desk, still in good view, would be on my neighbor's board in a classroom. Students are accustomed to smaller working surfaces than I, but the distraction of the classroom situation in which students are denied mobility and control of their working spaces must be considerable.

A pioneer investigation of lighting in more than 4,000 classrooms showed some interesting relationships between the health problems of the students and their location within the classroom. When the typical room was divided into quadrants, half the children with chronic infections were found at the rear left quadrant of the room, i.e., the rear quadrant nearest the back window. Were a line to be projected across the room from the front mullion at an angle of 40 degrees from the plane of the windows, some two-thirds of the children with nutritional problems would be found between this line and the windows. The severity of both kinds of problems increased from this line toward the rear left quadrant of the room.[17] The author attributes some of these results to the lighting within the rooms, but it is quite apparent that selection of seats as related to social and physical factors must also be taken into account.

All this made me wonder about the connection between classroom layout and student participation. The question seemed eminently researchable, since student participation could be objectively recorded, and there were many different sorts of classrooms available. Six rooms were finally chosen for the study. Two were seminar rooms that offered horseshoe or open square arrangements of chairs and two were laboratories that offered extreme examples of straight-row arrangements. The fixed tables with their Bunsen burners, bottles, and gas valves prevented any rearrangement of chairs. Of the other two rooms, one was windowless with starkly modern decor. To contrast with this "closed room" we selected another whose long wall was composed entirely of windows and which had been described by design students on campus as light and airy.

There were two discussion leaders (TAs), each responsible for three sections of approximately 25 students each. The TAs were told that "a study of discussion groups" would take place but nothing about specific details of the study. The professor knew the entire experimental plan and gave it his enthusiastic support. There were three observers, all undergraduate students, who attended the discussion sections and recorded student participation on prepared seating charts. The observers typically sat at the rear of a room and remained inconspicuous. These sections followed standard procedures of a typical

[17] D. B. Harmon, "Lighting and Child Development," *Illuminating Engineering*, XL (April 1945), 199–228.

class except that, in the middle of the semester, the students cha.. rooms. At that time they were informed that some of the sections had complained about the rooms and it seemed fair to switch in the middle of the semester. We were surprised and even saddened by how passively the students accepted the room changes. Accustomed as they are to IBM cards of seven different colors as well as arbitrary changes in faculty adviser, class hours, and course offerings, the students were able to accept a switch in rooms after the spring vacation with equanimity.

Our data were of two sorts, the first concerned the effects of rooms on student participation—was there more discussion in the seminar rooms than in the laboratory, more absenteeism in the windowless room, and so forth. The second concerned the *ecology of participation* or the way discussion varied as a function of location—were students in front more active than those in the rear; those in the center more active than those at the aisles? In the first instance we were comparing different rooms; in the second we were looking within each room. Comparison of rooms is of more relevance to value questions since we can determine if one room produced more discussion or fewer absences than another. Intraroom analyses involve the utilization of existing facilities by people willing to inhabit the environment but excluding those who choose to avoid it. Both questions are important to school administrators, the first in planning new facilities and the second in finding the best ways to utilize existing rooms.

All sections assigned to the seminar rooms and the open room met as scheduled, but escape behaviors were evident immediately in the laboratory and the windowless room. On the first day of classes in the laboratory, the TA handed a note to the department secretary requesting a change in room. When no action on his request was forthcoming, the TA moved his class to an empty room across the hall (also a laboratory but a more quiet one) where the class met for two periods. The second TA showed her distaste for the laboratory in comments to her students and in the fourth session moved her class outside with the avowed intention of meeting on the lawn from then on. Pressure from the professor induced her to meet in the assigned room. In the windowless room, escape behaviors were shown on two occasions. One TA brought his class outside but apparently did not find it very effective, so he met indoors after that. It is noteworthy that the students who followed the instructor out to the lawn arranged themselves in three straight rows in front of him. In the other section in the windowless room, the students officially petitioned the TA to meet outside. The request was written on the blackboard by the students, and the question was raised in class several times.

In the two seminar rooms an average of 9.0 students participated each session compared to 10.5 in the laboratory. This difference, which indicated more widespread participation in the laboratory, was statistically reliable. Although a higher proportion of people participated in the laboratory, there was a trend for greater absolute participation in the seminar rooms in terms of the larger total number of statements per class period. The implication is that a few people say more in a seminar arrangement, whereas participation is more widespread with the straight-row arrangement. There were no differences in participation between the open and the windowless rooms, nor were there significant differences between the sections in grades.

Table 5. Face-to-Face and Side Table
Participation in Seminar Rooms.

| | Average number of voluntary statements from | |
	Side tables (N = 226)	Table directly opposite instructor (N = 141)
Old seminar room 1st 6 weeks	1.63	2.42
Old seminar room 2nd 6 weeks	3.19	4.62
New seminar room 1st 6 weeks	2.89	3.69
New seminar room 2nd 6 weeks	0.88	1.97
Total: All rooms	2.08	3.15

SEMINAR ARRANGEMENT. We can now examine the way that participation was distributed in each room. With the seminar arrangement we can compare participation of students at the side tables with those sitting directly opposite the instructor. In every section in the seminar room there was more participation from people directly opposite the instructor than from those at the side tables. Students sitting away from the tables participated less than those at the tables. In the new seminar room, where the tables formed a hollow square, students avoided the chairs alongside the instructor. This was true even when the room was full—students sat on the floor or went out and secured new chairs. On the few occasions when a student occupied a chair adjacent to the instructor, he was generally silent throughout the entire period. This finding is in accord with the work on dominance relationships discussed in Chapter 2.

STRAIGHT-ROW ARRANGEMENTS. The laboratory, which had been included as an extreme example of a straight-row arrangement, was a challenge to the discussion leader. One TA typically sat at the front of the instructor's desk rather than behind it, and the other encouraged her students to bring their stools up to the front bench in an unsuccessful attempt to approximate a semicircular arrangement. The high tables and uncomfortable stools resisted her efforts, and a straight-row arrangement prevailed in all discussion sections meeting in this room. The students in the front row participated more than students in subsequent rows, but students around the walls participated more than students in any row but the first. This is also consistent with the eye-contact hypothesis, since only students in the front row and the sides had a clear and relatively unobstructed view of the TA.

In the open room, which contained four rows of chairs facing the instructor, students in the front row spoke more than students in the other rows, but this was not a reliable difference. The same was true of the windowless room—the first row again participated more, but this difference was not significant either. However, the data are complicated by the fact that latecomers in both rooms tended to sit in the front row. Our observers had noted that the front row, which was considered to be "too close" to the instructor in each room, was avoided by students who came on time. Of the 51 latecomers in these two rooms, 41 ended up in the front row, five in the second row, and five in the third row. When we removed the latecomers from the tabulations, we found the previous trends were accentuated and reached statistical reliability. Students in the first row participated more than students in either the second or the third rows. The layout here was the reverse of the laboratory where, because of the noise and high tables, the choice seats were in front. Of the 41 latecomers in the laboratory, 4 ended up in the first row, 1 in the second row, 17 in the third row, 10 in the fourth row, and 9 at the sides of the room. Removing the latecomers from the participation scores in the laboratory did not alter the trends. We still found 71 per cent of the students in the first row participating compared to approximately 50 per cent of the students in the other three rows. This suggests that the relationship between location and participation must take individual choice (environmental preference) into account. When the desirable seats are in front, increased participation results because the greater stimulus value of the instructor reaches the most interested students. When the favorable seats are in the middle or rear, the increased expressive value of the instructor for students in front will tend to cancel out the fact that the most interested students are in other rows, and there will be no clear relationship between row and participation.

Table 6. Participation by Row in Conventional Classrooms.

	Row 1 (N = 144)	Row 2 (N = 162)	Row 3 (N = 128)	Row 4 (N = 20)
	Average number of voluntary statements from			
Open room 1st 6 weeks	2.30	1.88	1.45	0.80
Open room 2nd 6 weeks	1.25	0.76	1.20	1.10
Windowless room 1st 6 weeks	1.00	0.78	0.97	—
Windowless room 2nd 6 weeks	2.38	1.57	1.78	—
Total: All rooms	1.77	1.23	1.32	0.95

The following year Joan Crawford repeated the study with a discussion group she was leading. By an interesting coincidence, her group also met in a small room where the front row was avoided by students. However, this time there were ample chairs in the rear rows and, throughout the semester, the front row was entirely empty. When we checked participation in rows two to six, there was a linear relationship between amount of discussion and proximity to the instructor. Students in the second row averaged 3.7 statements per session compared to 2.6 from those in the third row, 1.5 from those in the fourth row, and 0.5 from those in the fifth row.

Jan Ebert recorded class participation in two discussion sections, one in French and the other in freshman English. Students in the French class were allowed to sit where they pleased, but students in the English class were seated alphabetically. In the French class with voluntary seating, there was a clear connection between row and participation. The vast majority of voluntary statements and questions came from the first row. There was no difference between rows in the number of times a student was called upon by the instructor. In the English section with alphabetical seating, there was not much difference between the first two rows in voluntary participation, but the students in the third row participated very little. Again there was no difference between the three rows in frequency of being called on by the instructor. Miss Ebert's results support the idea that location and prior interest interact to affect class participation. When the most interested students sit where there is maximum visual contact with the instructor, there will be a clear connection between locations and participation, but when interested students are seated elsewhere, spatial effects will be less apparent.

A recent study by Levinger and Gunner[18] using a projective test, in which students arrange geometric forms and silhouettes on a felt background, showed that students who typically sat at the rear of a classroom placed greater distance between themselves and "a professor" than did students who sat at the front of the room. In the Netherlands Dr. M. J. Langeveld states:

> The seats chosen by the pupils themselves at the beginning of the school year give important social-psychological indications. For example, at the beginning of one school-year the following pupils "happened to" sit in the hindmost row: the only son of a widow who repeated this class, the only son of a widower, a heart patient who had been spoiled very much, a boy who is strongly inclined to withdraw from the school community, an older boy who had been sent away from another school, and two pupils repeating the class ages 20 and 21. And who occupies the front seats? The first three rows were occupied by five newcomers, the prefect of the class, a somewhat older boy who boards with one of the masters, three girls who have learned that they should work hard and pay attention, and three boys with the same attitude.[19]

A sensitive observer of student life in ghetto schools, Herbert Kohl advocates spatial freedom in the classroom. With freedom to move around and change seats, there is a continual shift in seating, but this, in Kohl's opinion, has not disrupted the fundamental fabric of the class. Rather the spatial freedom provides internal adjustments and compensations that avoid many possible disruptions. When feeling tense or anxious, a student might sit in the back row where he would be less likely to come into contact with others, but when he was interested in the material, he could come right up front.[20] Both Langeveld and Kohl illustrate the way that a perceptive teacher can use children's seating to gain information about the children and how they are feeling.

To test the expressive contact hypothesis that students in the center are psychologically closer to the instructor than students at the sides,

---

[18] George, Levinger and Jeannette Gunner, "The Interpersonal Grid: 1. Felt and Tape Techniques for the Measurements of Social Relationships," *Psychonomic Science*, in press.

[19] This section from Dr. Langeveld's book *Introduction to the Study of the Educational Psychology of the Secondary School* (Groningen-Batavia, 1937), p. 185 was translated and sent to me by Dr. Derk de Jonge.

[20] H. Kohl, *36 Children* (New York: The New American Library, Inc., 1967), p. 13.

we analyzed our participation data by dividing each room into a center zone and two side zones. The results from all ten sections showed that students in the center of a row participate more than students at the sides. Figure 5 shows pictorially that participation is greatest in the front row as well as within the center section of each row.

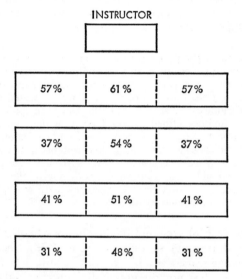

Fig. 5. Ecology of Participation in Straight-Row Classrooms.

Susan Tuana mapped participation in three large lecture halls with capacities of approximately 300 students. Each hall was divided into three sections, two smaller ones at the sides, and one larger in the center. She recorded participation in six different classes (ranging from drama to anatomy) meeting in each of the rooms. Her data, then, come from 18 independent observations of as many large classes. The number of questions asked per class averaged 2.3 (with a range of zero to nine), with a trend for questioning to decrease as class size increased. Almost half of the questions came from the two front rows in the center section (very few came from the front rows in the side sections), and another third came from students sitting along the side aisles. There was very little participation from the "faceless mass" in the middle areas. This is in accord with previous results since visual contact with the instructor is better in the front rows and along the aisles.

If we know little about what goes on inside classrooms, we know even less about what happens between classes, after class in school clubs, and to the student who does his homework as the radio on his dresser blares away. To understand the institutionalized learning process requires us to deal with a complex ecosystem that includes the community, the school building, as well as the classroom. Barker and Gump undertook one of the few studies in which the school itself was considered as an ecosystem. Comparing large and small high schools in the United States and England, they found that the impressive dimensions of the large school—the imposing exterior edifice, long corridors and countless rooms, the bustle of activity between classes, the masses of students, the complex table of organization of teachers and administrators—did not produce a richer learning environment than that at the smaller schools. Barker and Gump describe the small schools as small motors rather than large motors; they have all the essential parts of the larger motors, but fewer replications and differentiations of some parts. In the small schools there was more per capita participation in student government, school newspaper, drama, and musical activities.[21]

In this chapter we have omitted any discussion of learning outside the classroom. This schizophrenic posture is common to most design problems. While educational critics such as Edgar Friedenberg and Paul Goodman ask incisive questions about the relevance of contemporary education, school boards, principals, and teachers plan programs within existing structures. The basic module of school construction is the classroom containing a teacher and 20 to 30 students. At some future time the module may become the individual student in his study carrel equipped with teaching machine, TV unit, and various information retrieval devices connected to a central computer. We will then need conference rooms rather than lecture halls. At the present time, teachers are hindered by their insensitivity to and fatalistic acceptance of the classroom environment. Teachers must be "turned on" to their environment lest their pupils develop this same sort of fatalism.

[21] Roger G. Barker and Paul Gump, *Big School, Small School* (Stanford: Stanford University Press, 1964).

8

Designed for Drinking

Liquor is an important factor in the tourist business. A Wisconsin official complained that in sparsely populated wooded areas, where liquor licenses are few, promoters are reluctant to build resorts and vacation facilities, whatever the scenic charms may be. (*Landscape*, Winter 1966–67)

If a library is designed to encourage privacy and keep people out of each other's way, taverns are designed for just the opposite purpose. Anyone who walks through the door can partake of the companionable atmosphere as well as the available beverages. Pubs are by title public houses designed for sociability. Privateness, exclusiveness, and the ability to restrict entry are at a minimum. This is not true of all drinking places, such as private clubs which do restrict entry, but it is the special characteristic of the public house as an open region that makes it interesting to us from an environmental standpoint. No one tries to find privacy in a pub. One can find amusement and commodities that will change mood and relieve anxiety, companionship, and escape from family or office. However, the relief from stress or unpleasant interpersonal contact is not the same as privacy. Nor is the atmosphere due solely to the availability of alcohol, for the same condition was characteristic of many coffee houses. Indeed the teahouses of the Orient and the coffee houses of the Middle East bear many resemblances to the American tavern. Here is a poster from an old English coffee house:

> First, gentry, tradesmen, all are welcome hither
> And may without affront sit down together.

Pre-eminence of place none here should mind
But take the next seat that he can find.

The Viennese coffee house of today is described in these terms:

To many a Viennese his coffee house is his home away from home, his
haven and island of tranquility, his reading room and gambling hall,
his sounding board and grumbling hall. There at least he is safe from
nagging wife and unruly children, monotonous radios and barking dogs,
tough bosses and impatient creditors.[1]

Cafe patrons around the world may be in for an unpleasant surprise.
Furniture designer Henning Larsen was consulted by Copenhagen
cafe owners whose customers lingered endlessly over coffee. Larsen
developed a chair that exerts disagreeable pressure upon the spine
if occupied for over a few minutes. The Larsen chair is now being
marketed in New York and other cities. Hotel keepers and tavern owners have also been concerned with people being "too comfortable." This
is particularly true when they occupy public space without spending
money. When he took over the Waldorf Hotel, Conrad Hilton observed
that the comfortable divans were occupied day after day by the same
characters. Although they were correctly dressed and well-mannered,
they did not spend money in the hotel. Hilton remedied the situation
by moving the couches out of the lobby into the nearest food and
drink area of the hotel. In planning new hotels, the policy is to "make
the lounges small and the cafes big." [2]

The same view is held by those who design airport terminals, which
are perhaps the most sociofugal public spaces in American society.[3] In
most terminals it is virtually impossible for two people sitting down
to converse comfortably for any length of time. The chairs are either
bolted together and arranged in rows theater-style facing the ticket
counters, or arranged back-to-back, and even if they face one another
they are at such distances that comfortable conversation is impossible.
The motive for the sociofugal arrangement appears the same as that
in hotels and other commercial places—to drive people out of the

[1] Joseph Wechsberg, "The Viennese Coffee House: A Romantic Institution," *Gourmet* (December 1966), p. 16.

[2] Homer Bigart, "The Men Who Made the World Move," *Saturday Review* (April
22, 1967), p. 54.

[3] Sociofugal arrangements drive people toward the periphery of a room as contrasted to sociopetal arrangements, which focus people towards the center and
thereby bring them together. See Humphrey Osmond, "The Relationship Between
Architect and Psychiatrist," in *Psychiatric Architecture,* ed. Charles Goshen,
(Washington: American Psychiatric Association, 1959).

waiting areas into cafes, bars, and shops where they will spend money.

Dr. Johnson compared the public environment of a tavern with the private environment of a home where a guest cannot truly be at ease. A guest must always exert care and circumspection since the home is not his own. In the pub there is a general freedom from anxiety— any man with the money can be certain of a welcome. Paul Halmos describes the pub of this period as "the only free, non-esoteric, non-exclusive, weatherproof, meeting place for the ordinary worker." [4] Sherri Cavan, an American sociologist whose doctor's degree was based on her visits to San Francisco bars, describes public drinking places as *open regions*—people who are present, whether acquainted or not, have the right to engage others in conversation and the duty to accept overtures from them.[5] The concept was developed by Erving Goffman and goes beyond the obligation not to snub others, to the point where a person cannot be offended when someone else approaches him.[6] A patron can still arrange to be alone, bunching himself up at the end of the bar and staring down at his drink, or sitting at a remote table facing the wall, but these positions and postures must be maintained rigorously. Even this display of a desire for separation does not guarantee privacy, since at any time some sympathetic denizen may decide to initiate psychotherapy.

Cavan contrasts the lateral arrangement at the bar with the face-to-face arrangement at tables. The boundaries between individuals in rows are unclear and easier to cross than those of people seated around a table. At the bar one finds tendencies for encounters to be more fluid and unstable. The likelihood of interaction between strangers at a bar varies directly with the distance between them. As a general rule, a span of three bar stools is the maximum distance over which patrons would attempt to initiate an encounter. Any more than this would require raising one's voice to a level that would annoy other patrons. Cavan describes how interaction patterns vary between mixed sex and like sex pairs. Two men conversing with an empty stool between them are likely to remain that way since a move to adjacent stools would generally bring them too close to one another. However, if a man initiates a conversation with a woman at the bar with an empty chair between them, he is likely to move over to the adjacent stool in order to prevent someone else from coming between them.

There are numerous accounts of the connection between lighting, noise level, and duration of stay. It is reported that as illumination increases so does noise level, and both will reduce the amount of time

[4] Halmos, *op. cit.* p. 49.

[5] Sherri Cavan, *Liquor License* (Chicago: Aldine Publishing Company, 1966).

[6] Erving Goffman, *Behavior in Public Places* (New York: The Free Press, 1963).

people remain inside a drinking establishment. If a restauranteur wants to capitalize on high turnover, he uses high illumination levels and doesn't worry too much about soundproofing. On the other hand, if he wants people to remain a long time he uses dim lighting and sound-absorbing surfaces such as carpets, drapes, and padded ceilings. Low illumination will permit greater intimacy between couples and thereby increase seating capacity. The findings are reasonable and accord well with studies of sensory facilitation between modalities, but they also should be systematically verified.

Neither has there been much empirical confirmation of the view that "the casual drink tastes better in pleasant surroundings. The company seems friendlier if the room is congenial, the fire bright, and the host or his servants welcoming." [7] The influence of environment on drug effects urgently requires further study. Many of the avid believers in the psychedelic revolution insist that drugs should be taken in a setting with soft music, carpeted floors, dim lighting, and pleasant company. They attribute some proportion of "bad trips" to the unfortunate conditions under which the drugs are taken, e.g., a frightened young man alone in his apartment with the shades drawn, towels stuffed under the door, and a chair propped against the doorknob. Maslow and Mintz demonstrated that attractive surroundings would affect people's judgment of pictures and their mental outlook.[8] Since society has seen fit to legislate the decor of the tavern, the amount of outside advertising, and whether drinks can be served to people seated or standing up, the least that is needed is some factual information on the role of tavern milieu as it affects the drinker's outlook and behavior.

Whereas many people feel that environment facilitates the mood enhancing effects of alcohol, the obverse position that alcohol will aid in the appreciation of the environment is not widely accepted. Museum directors and national park authorities, to name only two groups, are generally opposed to the consumption of alcohol on the premises. Cavan cites the ruling of the California State Park Commission that "if the intent of the winter park authority is to provide access to an area of outstanding natural beauty and outdoor recreation, sale of liquor at the mountain station will not enhance this experience." [9] Actually there is very little information on the way that alcohol affects aesthetic experience apart from anecdotes and moral strictures. Park authorities and museum directors object less to the effects of alcohol on the view-

---

[7] A. Campbell, *The Book of Beer* (London: Dennis Dobson, n.d.), p. 235.

[8] Abraham Maslow and N. Mintz, "Effects of Aesthetic Surroundings," *Journal of Psychology,* XLI (1956), 247–54.

[9] Cavan, *op. cit.*

er's perception than on his behavior as it affects other people. Even if it were established that alcohol enhanced aesthetic experience, its role in this culture in automobile accidents and aggressive behavior might be sufficient to keep it out of culture palaces or recreation areas and confined to settings specifically designed for its use.

The physical form of the drinking establishment is as much a product of legal restrictions as economic laws and social customs. The field of tavern design reveals quickly the limitations of a purely functional approach to architectural problems. In New York City the public bar may not be the major feature of the establishment; in Saskatchewan a patron may not be served standing; in Alberta the beer parlor must close during dinner hour; public drinking places in Chicago must have an outside window that enables people outside to look in. It would be hazardous to design a drinking place without the assistance of local architects, beverage control officials, and city fathers; generally it is wise to bring them all into the act. Finding a place to drink or buying a bottle are two instances where interstate travel makes a real difference. One can eat the same food in a Holiday Inn anywhere, but he can order wine but not whiskey with his meal in one place, and in the next he must bring his own bottle and entrust to the waiter the onerous task of pouring it. Generally it is cheaper for a person to drink at home than in the local tavern. The *raison d'être* of the tavern goes beyond the opportunity for people to drink alcoholic beverages. This fact must be understood before one can understand the social and physical form of the tavern. A man goes to a bar to drink, to see and/or meet other people. It is a place to avoid boredom and existential loneliness. A bar allows for the transformation of loneliness into alienation with the availability of oblivion through alcohol.

Within the United States there are major regional and local differences in drinking places; within the same city there will be neighborhood taverns that draw their clientele from the surrounding blocks and downtown cocktail lounges that draw people from all over the city and beyond. The neighborhood pub will encourage sociability among regular patrons, but the outsider will be looked upon with suspicion and hostility. Such pubs are frequently called "locals" by regular customers. This is the situation in Ireland where each crossroads has its own cherished public house with a fiercely dedicated clientele. Frequently these are regarded as private preserves by the regulars, and the welcome mat is extended to visitors only if they are known to the regulars. An outside sign reading "Select" informs ladies to keep out.[10] A study of neighborhood taverns in Chicago by Gottlieb

[10] A. Kerr, "Fare Well in Erin," *Gourmet* (March 1967), p. 34.

showed that 83 per cent of the patrons resided within two blocks of the tavern in which they were interviewed.[11] On the other hand it is not difficult in any American city to find examples of the bar where meaningful contact is at a minimum. V. S. Pritchett describes the lonely men in New York City sitting speechlessly on a row of barstools, with their arms triangled on the bar before a bottle of beer, their drinking money before them.[12] If anyone speaks to his neighbor under these circumstances, he is likely to receive a suspicious stare for his efforts. The barman is interested in the patrons as customers—he is there to sell, they are there to buy. Another visiting Englishman makes the same point when he describes the American pub as a

> hoked up salon, the atmosphere is as chilly as the beer . . . when I asked a stranger to have a drink, he looked at me as if I were mad. In England if a guy's a stranger, it's automatic that each guy buys the other a drink. You enjoy each other's company, and everyone is happy.[13]

Yet even in England the complaint has been made that

> A good deal of drinking today is vertical and hurried: far too infrequently do we meet the place where you are welcome to sit comfortably round table or fire, talk and drink at your ease without a waiter hovering around, emptying the ashtrays, whipping away any empty bottles or glasses, as a mute reminder that it is about time you reordered.[14]

Another example of an isolated environment in New York City, probably overlapping in its clientele with the lonely New York bar, is the movie house showing pornographic films:

> As to that audience, regardless of time of day or night, weekday or weekend, it is composed of lone men who sit passively and patiently as far as possible in a geometric mosaic worthy of ninth-century architects. It is considered bad form to sit directly behind, or behind and one seat to the side, of an earlier arrival. And, in five or six trips, I never heard a patron address a single word to another patron.[15]

The pub owner is legally responsible for the acts of his patrons. He can lose his license if he serves people who are underage, drunk,

---

[11] David Gottlieb, "The Neighborhood Tavern and the Cocktail Lounge," *American Journal of Sociology*, LXII (1957), 559–62.

[12] Pritchett, *op. cit.*, p. 71.

[13] Tony Kirby, "Who's Crazy?" *The Village Voice* (January 26, 1967), p. 39.

[14] Campbell, *op. cit.*, p. 235.

[15] M. Valenti, "The Lonely Private World of Dirty Movies," *The Realist*, No. 63 (October 1965), pp. 5–6.

disorderly, gambling, engaged in lewd or lascivious behavior, or who establish liaisons for such acts in his place.[16] The liquor commissioners in Nova Scotia may "at their own discretion and for any reason they deem sufficient" suspend any license they have granted. Owners of theaters, bowling alleys, and hotels are also accountable for some acts of their patrons, but the range of offenses as well as the intensity of official scrutiny and enforcement are much more evident in drinking establishments. As one man wryly observed,

> the only person who would possibly succeed as an English publican is an unusually erudite and resourceful lawyer. . . . Considering the number of mistakes a [publican] can make, it's astonishing that there's ever time in the law courts for dealing with other matters, like murder and income tax evasion.[17]

Drinking establishments establish their own unique character, which will determine who will be attracted to the premises, how they will act, what they will drink, and how long they will stay. The bar that serves the young unmarried set will attract those who want to associate with young unmarried people—probably other young unmarried people. Jim Ghidella interviewed 48 patrons at "The Hut," a decrepit beer parlor in a university town, unique in that it was the only establishment there that did not attract students. The atmosphere was dingy, and the barstools were worn and patched. Almost all the patrons were white males of working class background. More than a third of those interviewed visited the establishment once or twice every day, and most of the remainder came once a week or more. Most of the regulars restricted their bar attendance to this particular place. They felt it was "an established place" which contained working people of their own age. Although four-fifths of the patrons came in alone, almost all made some contact with another person during their stay in the bar.

The sort of patron who prefers a low-key working class atmosphere does not object to drab surroundings. In fact, he prefers this to newer establishments. One cannot readily ask about the "functional environment" of a drinking establishment without knowing the prospective clientele. Whatever is built is likely to attract those individuals adapted to the establishment. Careful choice of location, external appearance, decor, and price list will influence who the patrons will be. This illustrates a fundamental difference between the architect's and the

---

[16] M. Thomas, *The Taproom Lawyer* (London: Chatto & Windus, Ltd., 1959), p. 11.

[17] F. A. M. Graham, "Pity the Publican," *Gourmet* (April 1968), p. 70.

biologist's ideas of functionalism. To a biologist a species is adapted when it fits into its surroundings—for example, when a bird beak is suitable for obtaining the sorts of seeds available in its biotope, however unusual or grotesque that beak may appear to zoo visitors. Biologists are generally concerned with things as they are, or the reasons why they developed as they did, rather than environments and organisms that do not yet exist. He is concerned with adaptation and habitat selection, whereas the architect is concerned with planning a new world.

To understand the connection between physical form, social custom, and legal regulations, I undertook a series of observations in beer parlors in Edmonton, Canada. The lowest common denominator of a Canadian beer parlor is that only beer can be purchased (by the glass or bottle), and it must be consumed on the premises. There are numerous variations of this theme, particularly in regard to the sale of food and the presence of women. Some years ago the Province of Alberta forbade men and women to sit in the same beer parlor—each hotel had two rooms, one for men and one for women. A man would escort his lady to the door of her beer parlor, make sure she found a seat, and then hasten back to the men's side, call the waiter over, and order for himself and his lady next door. The situation has improved somewhat, largely at the insistence of the hotel owners. There are still two sections in the Edmonton beer parlors, one for men and the other for ladies and escorts. If for some reason a woman wants to drink only in the presence of other women, she is out of luck. There were 32 beer parlors in Edmonton, a city of 350,000 in western Canada, in addition to about the same number of cocktail lounges, dining lounges, and private clubs. In contrast, Worktown, which was studied by the Mass Observation team, contained 304 pubs to service 175,000 people. The men's section of the Edmonton pub, which was the concern of our study, was a large open area containing tables, each surrounded by four chairs. No patron could be served standing, and singing and group games were forbidden.

A recent article describes the Canadian drinking man in these terms:

> It doesn't take a Sherlock Holmes to spot an English-Canadian tourist drinking abroad. . . . In a bar where everybody else is standing, the Canadian is the one sitting down. When it comes time to order another round, the Canadian is the one who compulsively drains his glass to the last drop before handing it back to the waiter. When the locals break into song, the Canadian looks ill at ease. The bright lights bother him a bit and so do all the signs exhorting him to drink this or that brew. . . . The reason Canadians tend to have a Pavlovian response to alcohol instead of regarding it as a relaxing pastime, must have some-

thing to do with the conditioning they receive in their native environment. They come, after all, from a country where a temperance ethos has been transformed into legalistic chaos, where public drinking is a solemn ritual conducted in stygian gloom. . . .[18]

We were particularly interested in the *isolated drinker*, the man who sits by himself and consumes beer in the presence of other people. If our ideas on the importance of the pub as a social center are correct, a lone drinker in a social setting deserves particular attention. The *solitary drinker*, who drinks by himself away from other people, usually in a private dwelling or rented room, has frequently been described as a prealcoholic. It seems important to distinguish between a man who drinks in solitude and one who drinks alone in a setting designed to encourage sociability. The isolation of the latter is more a matter of social than physical distance. Georg Simmel described it this way, "The feeling of isolation is rarely as decisive and intense when one finds himself physically alone, as when one is a stranger without relations, among many physically close persons, at a party, on a train, or in the traffic of a large city." [19] The situation of a man drinking beer by himself in the presence of others fits Simmel's concept of isolation. It is apparent that environmental programming must do more than establish proximity to facilitate communication and friendship.

During the first study, which took place in 1962, each of Edmonton's 32 beer parlors was visited twice. The sessions covered all the open hours. We were not interested in differences between individual pubs, and there were many, particularly when one compared neighborhoods, but rather in the total picture of beer parlors in the city.[20] The observer visited each pub at a specified hour and sat down at a table that afforded a clear view of some part of the beer parlor. The observer attempted to be as inconspicuous as possible and ordered the expected amount of beer, generally one large glass.[21]

The Mass Observation team had found that people in groups drink larger quantities than people alone and attributed this to the social pressure on a person in a group to keep up with the fastest member.[22] At first glance this view is supported by our findings that the average

[18] Marshall, *op. cit.*, p. 1.

[19] Georg Simmel, *The Sociology of Georg Simmel* (New York: The Free Press, 1950).

[20] Robert Sommer, "The Isolated Drinker in the Edmonton Beverage Room," *Quarterly Journal of Studies on Alcohol*, XXVI (1965), 95–110.

[21] Glass size was restricted by statute to small (11 ounce) glasses and large (22 ounce) glasses. All figures involving consumption are given in units of small glasses.

[22] Mass Observation, *The Pub and the People* (London: Victor Gollancz Ltd., 1943), p. 17.

number of new glasses ordered by isolated drinkers was 1.7 compared to 3.5 by group drinkers. Although it is clear that people in groups drink larger quantities than people alone, the implication of this trend becomes intelligible only when we examine the time spent in the pub by each person. We found that group drinkers, on the average, spent twice as long in the pub as isolated drinkers. This made it necessary to re-examine our figures on consumption taking into account duration of stay. This comparison shows no difference in the tempo of drinking by isolated and group drinkers. People in groups drink more than people alone, not because they drink faster, but because they remain longer. The presence of companions has less effect on the tempo of drinking than on the attractiveness of the pub as a place to sit.[23] One cautionary note is necessary: we have no way of knowing what happens to an isolated drinker when he leaves the pub. The fellow may simply go down the street to the next pub looking for the companionship that he did not find in the first place. Support for this notion comes from observation of loners who were joined by other people. Of the 29 joined isolates, 21 remained through the entire 60-minute observation period.

The total amount of beer consumed, regardless of whether the person was alone or in a group, varied directly with the length of time in the pub. People who remained less than 15 minutes (during the one-hour observation period) averaged 0.4 new glasses, people who remained between 16 and 30 minutes averaged 1.1 new glasses; people who remained 31 to 45 minutes averaged 2.8 new glasses; and people who remained 46 to 60 minutes averaged 4.9 new glasses. It is hardly surprising that people who stay longer in the pub drink more, but it is of interest that the oft-described pattern of "nursing" a single beer for an indefinite period is extremely rare in the Edmonton beer parlor. Of those people who remained longer than 45 minutes, and this includes both isolated and group drinkers, every single one ordered at least one additional glass.

A limitation of this study was its use of one-hour periods, which put a ceiling on the amount of drinking possible. We therefore embarked on another study to determine how long patrons stay in the pub and relate this to their drinking. During this second study, which

[23] Eugenia Butler decided to test the "gabby woman hypothesis" by seeing how long male and female college students remain in a college cafeteria. To her surprise, she found no difference between men and women, but there was a marked difference between students dining alone and those in groups. Students eating alone remained an average of 15 minutes, students eating with members of their own sex remained an average of 28 minutes, and students eating in mixed-sex groups remained an average of 34 minutes.

took place several months later, the observer arrived at a beverage room and selected as subjects those patrons who entered after he did. He was instructed to select three isolated and three group drinkers as subjects in each pub and remain as long as the subjects stayed. The median length of stay for isolated drinkers was 22 minutes, for group drinkers 54 minutes, and for joined isolates 89 minutes. Consumption of beer depended on the time a person remained in the pub—the longer a person stayed, the more he drank. As before, there was no difference in tempo of drinking between isolated, group, and joined isolate drinkers. The difference in total consumption was attributable solely to the length of time a person remained in the pub.

These results do not support the idea that the social stimulation of being a part of a drinking group increases drinking tempo. It is likely that this finding is due to the unique physical environment of the Edmonton pub, particularly since the Mass Observation team reported different results in Worktown. The patrons in an English pub can play darts or skittles, read the papers, watch the birdie, or take part in heated discussions of politics that include half the men in the pub. The English pub is much smaller, more intimate, and friendlier than the large Edmonton establishments where there is nothing to do but converse (if you happen to be sitting with someone else) and drink beer. Hot meals are not available, and there are practically no other diversions—television is restricted to special events, and then only with the permission of the Provincial authorities.[24] The lone drinker has nothing to do except drink and watch other people drink. The group drinker can talk with his tablemates and, with the stimulation from a beer, this is probably sufficient to keep him occupied. The fact that joined isolates stay longest supports the idea that the opportunity to meet others, rather than look at them (the spectator hypothesis) or the presence of beer, is what makes the pub a pleasant environment. The Spartan surroundings mean that social factors become preeminent in decisions to stay or leave. It is likely that diversions such as darts or cards would enable lone drinkers to remain longer, but we do not know how this would affect drinking. The Mass Observation team believed that these activities reduced the amount of drinking. They suggested that the high rate of arrests for drunkenness in another community, not the one they studied, occurred because the licensing authorities discouraged games and activities. The general belief among Albertans was that the Provincial government, which was known for its Fundamentalist views, reluctantly allowed drinking but attempted to make it as depressing as possible. When law and architecture con-

[24] Subsequent laws have changed this policy.

spire to inhibit sociability, a pub can be a place to buy and drink beer, but that is about all.

It is difficult to give a simple answer to the question: "What is the function of a drinking establishment?" There is reason to believe that the major function of a pub for most patrons is to provide a setting where people can come together—if not to meet at least to be with others—to maintain the *social distance* as the biologist Hediger uses the term. The patron may not be interacting with others, but at least he is not so far away that he has lost contact with his species. The key element here is being with other people in a particular sort of relationship, which can range from the friendliness of the neighborhood tavern to the coaction of the cocktail lounge where the availability of alcoholic beverages is an important but not always decisive element in the ongoing interaction. We can think of people's needs to consume alcoholic beverages and design efficient institutions for dispensing them (including vending machines!); we can also think in terms of people's needs to be with others of their species and design settings where this is possible. In America today these two needs are filled by the same institution—the tavern. This has many implications for social problems connected with alcohol—including the 50 per cent of arrests connected in some significant way with alcohol, or the 2 per cent of drinkers who are likely to have problems handling alcohol —as well as society's attitudes toward other mind-changing drugs such as marijuana or LSD. Other countries provide specialized institutions —the opium den or the tea pad—where drugs other than alcohol may be taken legally. Our society by its legal code has made alcohol the major mind-changing agent, and this, in turn, has affected the evolution and form of the drinking establishment.

This is one reason why it is impossible to understand the physical form of the tavern, the arrangement of the furniture and the social relationships among the clientele without taking into account the laws and administrative rules surrounding alcohol consumption in our society. It is true that the design of the bathroom is influenced by building codes, union regulations, and cultural taboos but even here one does not find the detailed regulation that surrounds alcohol use. No functional approach could explain why one liquor store resembles a post office where a customer cannot touch the merchandise and another a pleasure palace. With alcohol use we deal less with a silent language than with the effects of explicit laws and restrictions.

9

Scholars in the Hotel Business

Daphne has a private penthouse room with a gorgeous view of the mountains from her balcony. Her suite is carpeted wall-to-wall, lavishly draped, beautifully appointed with cherrywood furniture and fully air-conditioned. She has a private bath and maid service. Is she an internationally known woman journalist living in the Swiss Alps or a jet set socialite residing in a lavish Paris hotel? No . . . Daphne is a typical all-American college freshman, living at the College Inn dormitory, University of Colorado. (*Institutions Magazine*, March 1967)

College dormitories are particularly interesting to us for two reasons: first, the necessity to take into account the student culture in questions of design and decor, and second, the large amount of behavioral data that has been collected but not used. Unlike schoolchildren, ladies in an old folks' home, or beer parlor patrons, college students will significantly rearrange and personalize their rooms to suit their needs. College housing also differs from most building forms in that literally thousands of studies of user satisfaction have been completed. As I delved into accounts of what was known about suitable accommodations for students, I continually encountered references to unpublished studies, mimeographed reports, masters theses, or simply second-hand reports of someone else's experiences. Whether one was talking about an obscure state college or about M.I.T., there were people in the housing office, sociology department, or counselling services who had been concerned with conditions in the residence halls. Typically this took the form of a survey of student opinion about present accommodations. It was also common to find surveys of room-mate satisfaction, the reasons why people moved out of dormitories, or coed living. Almost all the reports lay buried in obscure folders and files. People were unaware of work that had been done on their own campuses several years earlier. A problem in comparing these various studies is that the architectural elements and concepts are spe-cific to one campus and not directly comparable across settings. Some-times the same area is given different labels (e.g., study room, study library, quiet room, or library), and other times one finds areas serving different functions given the same name (e.g., both an active recreation area and a formal carpeted room are described in the house plans as "lounge areas"). The lack of an accepted vocabulary for residence halls makes it very difficult to tie together the results of different studies and even to compare different halls. Furthermore, what does it mean to know that students prefer single rooms if they cost a third more than double rooms? How does one apply experiences of Harvard graduate students to a freshman dorm in Wisconsin? Since complaints die down after a few months, does it really matter what is provided for students? These questions must be answered lest we amass still more "interesting" but irrelevant data.

Probably the major reason for the continued interest in college housing is its accessibility to researchers in design and the social sci-ences. For architecture students it remains the closest design problem at hand. Permission to enter the setting and question people is easy to obtain, and for budding sociologists and anthropologists it is a natural laboratory in social relationships. One can study the emergence of friendships from the very outset, the development of cliques and special interest groups, and the mass hysteria of football rallies and spring orgies. A second reason for the increased interest in college housing is the public consciousness of the importance of higher education and its place in society. Clark Kerr forecast that the knowledge industry would soon be the number one consumer of goods and services.[1] There is a vast amount of money going into college housing each year. It is now possible for a college to forecast its housing needs ten or more years ahead, which permits more rational and detailed planning than was possible when units were added singly as funds became available. A college need no longer wait for a wealthy alumnus to die before build-ing its dormitories; they can now be financed out of operating revenue. This has removed one of the most serious obstacles to intelligent dormitory planning.

Like so many of the topics we have discussed, the crucial questions

---

[1] Clark Kerr, interview, *Psychology Today* (October 1967), pp. 25–29.

about student housing begin with "why" rather than "how." We are in the midst of a virtual revolution in thinking about residence halls. Traditional assumptions about college housing are being challenged by private builders, architects, and student rebels. The student challenge is perhaps the easiest of the three to understand so we will deal with it first. In all areas of student life, including housing, students reject the idea that a university stands *in loco parentis*. With a surprising degree of maturity and sophistication, they question why any single institution of society, whether it be the police, the church, or the dean's office, should have the moral and legal authority to act toward them as parents. Certain areas of his life, the student believes, are his private business. It should be none of his landlord's concern if he has female visitors, a bottle of wine, or friends from out of town camped in their sleeping bags for a few days.

On some campuses, students have taken the lead in examining residence hall policies and their implications. The Student Employees Union at the University of Michigan published a hard-hitting report on housing available in the Ann Arbor area. The skills acquired by students in economics and sociology classes were used to the full. The students established that housing in Ann Arbor was grossly overpriced with landlords having a net return three or four times the yields of landlords in Detroit, Cincinnati, or other nearby cities. Students were typically required to take a 12-month lease which meant a subletting loss of 20 per cent in the summer months. From an analysis of advertisements, it was clear that competition between Ann Arbor landlords was based, not on lower rents or superior study facilities, but on various frills. Advertisements for apartments described spacious patios, terraces, pine walls, screened porches, sundecks, twin air-conditioners, two telephones, wall-to-wall carpeting, piped-in music, sunporches, French doors, bay windows, heated swimming pools, but no mention of study facilities.[2]

In England the National Union of Students published several reports on student accommodations. Instead of housing that is intended solely for university students, they recommend accommodation for students from a wide variety of institutions—technical schools, teachers colleges, as well as universities. This will require the sort of planning that exists in Sweden where the Central Students Council, representing proportionately all the educational institutions in Stockholm, elects a building committee comprised of students, faculty, and architects. The English students have been less concerned with the enforcement of

---

[2] University of Michigan Student Employees Union, "The Housing Problem," Ann Arbor, mimeo., n.d.

detailed building standards than with the quality of life from the standpoint of student needs. One of their recent reports defined the goals of student housing as follows:

1. To provide shelter for the student and his books.
2. To allow for privacy and facility for quiet study.
3. To surround the student with opportunities for comradeship.[3]

It is interesting to compare the reports of the National Union of Students with that of their American counterpart at Michigan or on our own campus. The English students take a broader view of the university as part of a larger social and economic system, they see universities in competition with, for example, urban redevelopment plans that would wipe out the large old houses that provide many students with lodgings. American students are more likely to seek out immediate enemies—the avaricious landlords or the puritanical dean of women— rather than to consider student housing as it is affected by changes in the larger society. The reason why built-in furniture is included in so many American dormitories, even though it is antagonistic to the goals of flexibility and personalization, is that it can be included in the initial mortgage loan from the Federal Government at a low interest rate, whereas detached furniture must be financed separately. Students who are unaware of such financial policies are unlikely to make much of a contribution to improved student housing. All too frequently the reason why dormitories are built as they are has more to do with financial considerations than with student or university needs.

Across the country private builders are entering the dormitory field. The largest builder of residence halls in the nation is Commercial Investment Trust Educational Buildings, Inc. This is a private firm that claims it can construct residence halls within a year without any capital outlay on the part of the institution. Several lavishly illustrated brochures show the floorplans and outsides of dozens of dormitories they have erected. Although most of these are of the conventional double room variety, exciting developments are occurring in the area of luxury housing. Perhaps luxury should be placed in quotes, but these private apartment buildings and residence halls are much closer in appearance to luxury hotels than to the drab residence halls known to an older generation of students. The lounges, corridors, and rooms are carpeted, there are swimming pools and sauna baths, bowling alleys, beauty parlors, and bookstores—in fact, everything one would

[3] National Union of Students, "Report on Student Housing," London, mimeo., n.d.

expect to find at a resort. The rents are only slightly above what is paid in university accommodation. By doubling up in an apartment or having three girls instead of two, the rent may be brought down below campus rates.

There is no consistent attitude among university administrators toward private dormitories. Some have welcomed their development on the grounds that they are now freed from devoting time, effort, and worry to a nonacademic matter that should never have been their concern in the first place. This is in line with the continental model of a university that is responsible for academic matters but not for the students' extracurricular life, which includes his eating, sleeping, and social activities. Where this philosophy has been adopted by the college authorities, it is not always accepted by the students' parents who still believe, rightly or wrongly, that the college is looking after Susie's welfare even if she does live in a downtown apartment.

Some university officials have tried to discourage the use of luxury apartments by students. This attitude has been interpreted as a manifestation of the puritanism and asceticism still prevalent in academic circles. There are professors who believe that students should undergo privation and suffering as a test of endurance. One need only look at the advice given to students on the proper study environment. In how-to-study books one finds statements like these: "Choose a straight-backed chair rather than a very comfortable one";[4] "All of the votes are in favor of a simple, rugged, straight-backed chair with no cushions. You study best when you're not too comfortable or relaxed. . . . For obvious reasons, avoid studying on a couch, easy chair, or in bed";[5] and finally, "A bed is no place to study. Neither is a sofa, nor a foam rubber lounge chair. When you become too relaxed and comfortable physically, your concentration also relaxes. A straight-backed wooden chair is best for most students; it allows them to work at maximum concentration for longer periods." [6]

When the authors made these admonitions, were they sitting bolt upright in straight-backed chairs at their desks? I am afraid that the answer will forever elude us. However, we have been able to assess the validity of these recommendations, and it is not very high. In one study we visited dormitory rooms on eight different campuses to interview students about their study habits. Among the things we ascer-

[4] M. J. Youle-Whyte, *Secrets of Studying* (Lincoln, Nebraska: Cliff's Notes, Inc., 1963).

[5] A. Lass and E. Wilson, *The College Student's Handbook* (New York: David White Company, 1965).

[6] C. E. Woodley, *How to Study and Prepare for Exams* (New York: Signet Books, 1961).

tained were: (a) whether the student had been studying just before the interview, (b) the specific place of study, and (c) his grade average. It was clear from the outset that only a small amount of studying took place at the student's desk. This trend was most marked in apartment-type halls where couches were available. In one such unit, only one out of six persons studying was sitting at the desk. Among nonstudiers —students who were just talking, lounging, or reading casually, the figure went down to one in 25.[7] A recent ad for phonographs reads: "Most of these students have stereo phonographs of their own. Why do they bring their favorite records to Pete's room?" Underneath there is a photograph of five students sprawled around the dormitory room. Two are sitting on one bed, another is on a second bed, one is squatting on the floor, and another is in a lounge-type chair. No one is sitting at the straight-backed chair, which remains forlornly at the desk. These results would not be so important except that the myth of the straight-backed chair is part of dormitory planning and regulations. A survey published in June 1967, conducted at 30 selected colleges and universities, reported that "the typical desk chair was constructed of wood without cushioning or springs."[8] On my own campus, there are no lounge chairs in the dormitory rooms. A regulation that freshman girls, for their first six months in the residence hall, must work at their desks for several hours a night has just recently been rescinded. A girl could have been censured and her "privileges" lost if she were, for example, reading on her bed or working her math problems on the floor. This is an instance of a myth about study environment becoming codified into, not only dormitory purchasing policies, but the regulations that govern user behavior. A final note on this particular study is that there was no difference in the grade averages of those students who had been working at their desks and those who had been working on their beds. There were as many honor students in one group as in the other.

There are also arguments against private accommodations based on the British tradition that residence halls are integral parts of a university experience. The newness of private dormitories prevents any assessment of their role in fostering academic community. We have found, for example, that the swimming pool at a local student apartment house serves as a social center for the residents. We were surprised at the small number of people sitting around the pool who actually went into the water. The pool served the same function as an

[7] Robert Gifford and Robert Sommer, "The Desk or the Bed?" *Personnel and Guidance Journal*, May 1968, pp. 876–78.

[8] Donald L. Finlayson, "Furbishing the Typical Residence Hall," *Student Housing Research* (June 1967), pp. 1–2.

Italian piazza or a neighborhood park. There was more social activity around the pool than we ever saw in dormitory lounges. At a fraternity house we surveyed, the kitchen was the main social and study center.

I believe that the major justification of college-owned housing must come under the heading of academic community. If the students get no more from a campus residence hall than a room or apartment downtown, there seems little reason why university authorities should concern themselves with a nonacademic matter. There are several programs in campuses around the country to bring cultural events, seminars, and classrooms into the residence halls.[9] Younger faculty are being asked to serve as tutors in the dormitories, but this program has not been overly successful in the larger universities where younger faculty are concerned with research and professional advancement and tend to place a high premium on their individual privacy. Students themselves are not always overjoyed to have a faculty member living among them; it smacks too much of the old authority-surveillance system.

We interviewed 72 freshman girls who had applied for dormitory housing but had been rejected because of a shortage of space, and a matched group of 72 girls in the dormitories. Four-fifths of the rejects were disappointed at first, but most were pleased at the way things turned out. More than three-quarters of the dormitory girls reapplied for campus housing the following year, but this was true of only 12 per cent of the girls who had lived off-campus for a year. The finding indicates that whereas one can grow to like dormitory living, it becomes less attractive to people exposed to other types of housing. There were no important differences between the dormitory and off-campus girls in terms of sickness, classes cut, or scholastic average. The major differences were in terms of school spirit and activities. Twice as many dorm residents were active in clubs and activities as off-campus girls and only 11 per cent of the dormitory girls felt isolated from the campus compared with 40 per cent of the girls living off-campus.

Any evaluation of college housing forms must begin with the realization that different sorts of students have different sorts of needs. One does not, for example, design the same facilities for graduate students as for undergraduates. There is even a highly significant difference between graduate students in zoology, sociology, and history, and professional students in law, medicine, and dentistry. Graduate students tend to be loners in their study and work habits, professional students cluster together. Medical students enter in a cohort, take the

[9] H. C. Riker, *College Students Live Here* (New York: Educational Facilities Laboratories, 1961).

same classes and exams at the same times, and generally finish their studies together. Graduate students have very little identification with any cohort, they take different classes (or no classes at all), and they are busy on their individual projects at the laboratory or library. Professional students like the idea of a law or a dentistry house where chores will be done on a cooperative basis. This is not as true for graduate students who are on separate schedules. Foreign students, too, have needs different from those of their American counterparts.

It should be apparent that the same facilities will not suit introverts and extroverts, lone and group studiers, people who need absolute quiet and those who require music while they study. There is no such thing as an optimal study environment for all students. We have conducted extensive interview and observational studies of how students read and study. Some retreat to the farthest part of the library stacks and work by themselves, and others prefer large reading rooms where other people are working around them. In a study hall, there is always a steady level of activity to mask any single action, but in the stacks every little sound or movement stands out. There are also students who study in the cafeteria, the music listening room, and the campus bowling alley. Knowing the working habits of writers and artists makes this understandable. One writer will work at his desk from 9:00 to 11:00 every morning and write his quota of 1,000 words, but the second needs to walk into the desert or sit at the rear of his favorite bar.

There are two basic methods by which a diversity of student needs can be met—flexibility and variety. The first is to provide flexible facilities, a dormitory environment that is responsive to individual needs. A start in that direction is being made by the planning group that, under contract to the University of California, is developing a dormitory shell whose internal dimensions can be varied quickly and economically. Over a weekend or Christmas vacation, rooms can be changed from single to double, or become four- or eight-man suites. The second method is to provide a variety of facilities that will maximize the student's range of choice. At the beginning of a year, students can select among accommodations that include apartments (with and without cooking facilities), high-rise or low-rise cluster units, with a further choice of single rooms, double rooms, or suites. The student is able to meet his individual needs through a combination of selection and adaptation.

Lack of recognition of these processes is another weakness of most existing housing studies. One cannot readily compare the average grades of fraternity men, apartment dwellers, and residence hall students if these are different people to start with. Furthermore, there are larger differences between individual fraternity houses than an over-all difference between fraternities and residence halls. If we want to know how a residence hall affects students, we will have to go inside the hall itself and observe student behavior. It will also be necessary to adopt an ecological perspective since the availability of facilities elsewhere—study halls as well as recreation areas—will affect what happens in dormitories.

Some educators pursue the question of optimal study environments by correlating college grades with the size of the student's desk, the availability of good lighting, access to a typing room, library facilities, and so forth. On the basis of our own research, this approach does not appear too fruitful. When his desk is too small or is inconvenient, a student will use his bed, the floor, or the library. What we find with inadequate facilities is not lower grades, but less use of the facilities and a consequent overutilization of things intended for other purposes. We must conceive of problems in terms of man-environment systems rather than of isolated pieces of furniture and structures.

Table 7 shows the results of visits to several dormitories at a private college in the Bay Area. As the number of room occupants increases, the likelihood that anyone will study decreases. A room that is pleasant and airy with one or two occupants may be stuffy, noisy, and unpleasant with six. We have been struck by the changing character of college libraries at different times of the year. There are some students who regularly study at the library in the evening for the quiet and solitude. However, during exam time these same students remain in their rooms rather than go to the noisy and crowded library.

Table 7. Studying as Related to Number of
Students Present in Double Rooms.

Number of people in room	Number of students	
	Studying	Not studying
1	12	8
2	8	11
3	0	11
4–5	1	9

We have also been concerned with improving privacy in dormitory living. However, privacy means many things to many people and varies from one occasion to another. Sometimes it means being absolutely alone and away from all people, at other times it means being intimate with a single person but away from all others, and sometimes it includes the anonymity and impersonality of a large city where one is free to do as he chooses. That privacy for dormitory residents was largely a matter of visual protection became clear during several surveys of converted army barracks that have served as "temporary" student housing for some decades. Although the barracks were unappealing from an aesthetic standpoint, they were favored by students because, for one thing, they were the only dormitories on campus with single rooms. The one item on a list of 20 for which these barracks were rated excellent was privacy, whereas they were rated as "terrible" in regard to soundproofing. The walls were typical barracks construction, and one could hear conversations or noise from adjoining rooms. However it was still easier for a girl to gain auditory privacy by talking low in her single room than for a girl in a double room to gain visual privacy from a physically present roommate.

Further support for this interpretation came from a second survey we undertook the following year when the barracks were closed to student occupancy. The former residents were dispersed to other dorms and off campus. Miss Connie Mahoney, one of the former residents, contacted and interviewed as many of these girls as she could. Most had moved to modern dorms with double rooms or apartments. The second survey made it clear that soundproofing had improved for the better—only one girl felt it now needed major improvement compared to two-thirds of the students the previous year. On the other hand, privacy was worse than it had been in the barracks. Previously two-thirds of the girls had rated it as excellent compared to 12 per cent the following year. Since the accommodations were now more

Table 8. Ratings of Privacy and Soundproofing
in Single and Double Rooms.

	Excellent	Satisfactory	Needs minor improvement	Needs major improvement
Ratings in barracks with single rooms				
Privacy	17	8	1	0
Soundproofing	0	2	7	16
Ratings in modern dorms with double rooms				
Privacy	3	19	2	0
Soundproofing	7	8	8	1

substantial, modern, and attractive in virtually every respect, the most logical reason for this decline in privacy was the change from single to double rooms. In this situation at least, privacy was virtually independent of noise levels (see Table 8). Undoubtedly one can find situations in which this is not true, as in the case of teenagers who use their transistor radios to gain privacy by surrounding themselves with a curtain of sound, but in dorm living privacy seems mainly a matter of visual rather than of auditory protection.

A dormitory room must fill many different sorts of needs. One cannot think of it solely as a study place. It is also the student's sleeping area and in most cases his major social space. As an undergraduate I spent more time talking to other students in my room than in any of the "lounges" on campus. In this age of changing functions one rarely designs an area for a single fixed function or a fixed number of occupants. Flexible buildings whose internal dimensions can be varied overnight are one solution to the problem. The other common solution is to provide different sorts of spaces that can be used as needed. The design of the cars for the Bay Area Rapid Transit is intended to take into account the needs of both upper-middle-class commuters as well as rush hour sardines. Planners of the project believed that unless they could attract upper-middle-class riders from the suburbs, the project would be doomed economically. However, the same cars would have to serve the needs of the masses in the city center. The solution was to design a car with small conversational areas surrounded by open spaces with the hope that the former would provide a degree of intimacy and comfort for the commuters on their long journey and the open areas would satisfy the standing hordes during the rush hour. The same kind of solution has been recommended in dormitory planning. Some colleges have tried to separate social, study, and sleeping areas, but there is little evidence of how this works in practice. Conceivably the use of poor lighting in the bedroom could drastically curtail its use as a study place, but whether this is in the student's interests is an important question. There is a further point that many students like to study together. This cannot be done properly in either the social area (too noisy) or the study lounge (disturbing to others). Unless one wants to have a special room for this sort of function, too, and for every other conceivable function, he would probably be better off with "loose fitting space" that can be used for a variety of activities, relying on the student's adaptive capacity to seek out other more suitable spaces when needed.

One must also take into account the norms of the student culture. It is not sufficient to have soundproof walls if gregarious residents will not respect a closed door. Even those halls without viable cultures have miniature societies and cliques. The difference between a culture and a society is that a culture implies something enduring over time that produces artifacts, traditions, legends. The notion is more fitting for fraternities where present members and alumni control future membership than in the dormitories where entrance is open to all applicants. One still finds that some dormitories develop reputations for participation in campus activities or for being good study places or social centers. Once these reputations take hold, future applicants, at least among continuing students, weigh this information in making their choices the following year so there is some self-selection among dormitory residents, too. Although one can discuss the dorm culture apart from the physical structure of the buildings or the personalities of the residents, they are all intrinsically connected. The use of carpeting, for example, can significantly affect the atmosphere of a school building. Reports of teachers and administrators (although more systematic data are needed) indicate that elementary and high school students act differently in carpeted hallways and classrooms. Recent newspaper descriptions of the new Montreal subway indicate that local residents respect the attractive surroundings, and the daily litter for the entire Metro system is measurable in pounds, whereas in the New York subways it is weighed in tons. The physical environment of a building creates certain expectations about how one should act— people lower their voices and stop smiling when they enter banks and churches.

This dimension of *connotative meaning* must be taken into account by designers. The landscape architects working for the State of California have a problem: people keep making off with picnic tables and benches. The solution has been to design heavy concrete furniture, but vandals persist in carting away the concrete blocks. Serious thought is being given to more formidable furniture with chains, ground anchors, and embedded concrete. Such a solution is self-defeating— the greater the efforts at security, the more demeaning is the situation in the eyes of the user. The most efficient and economical long-range solution is to change public attitudes by providing good furniture that citizens can respect and protect. Arguments that littering, vandalism, and thievery necessitate intense security measures prove expensive and self-defeating in the long run. When people are given nice things and learn how to use them, they will take care of them. The occasional psychopath or thief can be apprehended, and the citizens will help the police when the property elicits respect. They will applaud the vandal when the ponderous concrete bench is another reminder of their degradation. The argument applies with equal force to city parks, prisons, and college dormitories. The culture of the users must be understood and respected.

We turn now from a consideration of specific building types such as schools and hospitals to the designer's fantasy—the totally planned optimal environment. No longer are there constraints of law, custom, and ignorance; everything is planned in the best way possible. Hamstrung as they are by laws, traditions, superstition, and insensitivity, it is not surprising that designers dream of Utopia.

10

Utopia

There was another dream, a quite impossible dream, we'd turn yearningly to, years ago. The tantalizing dream of a tropical island where the sun *always* shone, where the tradewind touched the skin with gentle balm, where the water was blue, the sand soft, the land *always* green. A remote dream then. But today, when the swiftness of travel has turned hours into minutes and giant jets touch down on new, palm-fringed airstrips, the magic islands of the incomparable Caribbean have become as close and as attainable as your country cottage and infinitely more wondrous. (Advertisement)

In 1516 Sir Thomas More described an imaginary island called Utopia which enjoyed perfection in politics, law, and family relations. More's choice of name was not accidental and came from the Greek *ou* (not) and *topos* (a place) to emphasize that Utopia did not and probably could not exist, although it was an ideal toward which men could strive. Americans conceive of Utopia as an ideal form of social organization, since this is where our problems lie, but less advanced people think of having all the material conditions necessary for survival. The American Utopia rests on spatial segregation and involves at every turn arguments of the rights of the minority as opposed to the will of the majority. One cannot discuss Utopias without examining the pros and cons of segregation. It should be noted that the term itself, which has a literal meaning of "set apart," does not indicate whether the people themselves seek apartness or whether it is forced upon them.

Chad Walsh laments the declining number of authors who construct ideal societies along More's lines compared to those who foreshadow nightmares that he labels Dystopias, inverted Utopias, and anti-Utopias.[1] These portrayals of an unwholesome future were only a minor satiric fringe of the imaginary society literature in the nineteenth century, but they are the dominant type today. It is possible to view these anti-Utopias as warnings that society is on the wrong course. As such, they serve a positive function, much the same as anxiety does for the human body. The totally alienated individual does not write books.

Even the word Utopia has fallen on bad times. A design can be dismissed peremptorily by calling it Utopian, which means, in plain language, unrealistic, impractical, and expensive. The planner Doxiadis substitutes the term Entopia, or "in place," which is realizable, for Utopia, which is not.[2] This is a pluralistic society of competing and opposed interests in which one man's Utopia will not be another's. This can produce a superordinate notion of Utopia as a society that achieves the most equitable balance of individual prescriptions for the good life. No one gets exactly what he wants, but no one is completely dissatisfied either. Probably the most common notion of Utopia is what might be called the visionary environment—the furthest application of the most advanced technology. It is a Buck Rogers world with floating cities covered by plastic globes, people flying effortlessly through purified air, and all food and clothing manufactured in spotless factories where machines do all the work. This is a familiar scene to science fiction readers, and it remains a pleasant enough fantasy until questions are raised regarding the quality of life for the inhabitants. Then one finds the Dystopias of Orwell and Huxley.

American writers are less concerned now than they were several decades ago with spatial mobility as a means of finding Utopia since it has become apparent that there are problems in the best places too, usually produced by the attractiveness of the best places for too many people. Kansans and Oklahomans still dream about the Golden State of California, but they are aware of the smog, traffic, and high living costs. If a place is desirable, it will attract people until the point is reached at which the density produces undesirable consequences that cancel out its advantages. California's northern coast is still unspoiled, but below Mendocino the entire coastline is for sale. Places where subdivisions spring up overnight are within an hour's drive from the Bay Area megalopolis and provide desirable second homesites. The lack of

[1] Chad Walsh, *From Utopia to Nightmare* (New York: Harper & Row, Publishers, 1962).

[2] C. A. Doxiadis, "The Coming Era of Ecumenopolis," *Saturday Review* (March 18, 1967), pp. 11–14.

good roads, industry, or agriculture above Mendocino means that few people can earn their living in this area. It could conceivably be a retirement zone, but the wind, fog, and wild surf do not appeal to most older people. So long as this situation continues, the northern coast will remain resistant to human settlement. the construction of a four-lane highway to replace the hairpin curves and sheer cliffs of Route 1 might bring San Franciscans another 50 miles up the coast, but the residents of Rockport, California, are safe for another 25 years, unless of course an instant city takes shape around a NASA station.

Natural law will in time void any environmental Utopia so far as human settlement is concerned. The National Parks and Wilderness Areas preserve wondrous places to visit and explore, but the major reason why these places are still worth visiting is the law restricting human settlement. Not only will a good place attract people to an undesirable degree, but the reverse can happen, too. When people leave a setting because of a harsh climate or difficult economic situation, it can then become desirable as a land of open sky with plenty of breathing room.

Historians and sociologists have shown a fascination toward Utopian communities. One reason is the manageable scale, making social process and all its ramifications clearly visible, and the origin of the community traceable in space-time. American Utopian communities have been of three sorts: religious, nonsectarian, and factory towns. The second category, the nonsectarian and frequently communistic society, has attracted the bulk of the attention although the number of inhabitants in the religious communities and the mill towns starting with Lowell, Massachusetts, on up to the new industrial cities such as Kitamet, British Columbia, have housed far more people and have proved more viable economically and politically.

The internal use of space within Utopian communities is often very different from outside society. Communitarians of the secular variety are characterized by close physical contact and directness of manner. Visiting Synanon or Kerista one is struck by the freedom from taboos against body contact. There is also a directness of gaze, a process of continual confrontation, that makes the visitor uncomfortable until he gets used to it. Hippies complain that "squares" do not look at one another, they treat each other as nonpersons. At Big Sur Hot Springs one might see a man and a woman discovering one another at breakfast, embracing for no special reason—even before the coffee is served. A female reporter intent upon writing a story about the Keristans, a communitarian love cult in New York City, "found herself being groped by both sexes. The groping was impersonal and almost mechanical, as though this were an habitual form of communication." [3] This description does not fit most religious communities, specifically those founded as a reaction against the licentiousness and immorality of the outside world. Yet the line between these subtypes is not always obvious. A nominee to the California State Board of Education objected to schools teaching about the Pilgrims because "they lived in a communistic society."

The concept of Utopia as well as the word itself is surprisingly frequent in architectural books and articles. It seems to fill much the same role for architects as does health for medical practitioners and efficiency for engineers. As laymen continue to strive toward a Utopia through laws intended to produce harmonious and frictionless social intercourse, designers use environmental programming to develop physical forms that will increase the sum-total of human happiness. The problem is generally phrased in quasi-scientific terminology, such as the quest for the optimal environment. Some opportunity for planning on a Utopian scale is provided in the design of New Towns, instances where a city arises whole according to a prearranged plan. In theory such New Towns are balanced communities that provide jobs for the residents although there may be some commuting in and out. Specifically excluded from this category are the suburban bedroom communities whose residents work outside the community and whose workers (plumbers, gardeners, teachers) cannot afford houses in the community and live elsewhere. Perhaps because of the American antipathy toward large-scale planning, the development of New Towns in the United States has lagged far behind many European countries.

Another fertile field for Utopian planning is the design of special facilities for the blind, crippled, or the insane, although phrasing the problem in this way tends to convert the clients into nonpersons. There are excellent studies of the effective turning radius for a wheel chair, the optimal incline of a stairway, or the best sorts of railings for showers and baths that have proven invaluable in designing facilities for the handicapped. Some planners, discouraged by their lack of success in finding optimal environments for healthy middle class families, are beginning to maintain that their *raison d'être* is the design of facilities for people with special needs—low educational achievement, blindness, or insanity. Not only are these needs definable, but the people themselves are usually helpless or dependent and thus unable to protest the planner's intervention into their lives. The poor and the disabled become the guinea pigs of social and environmental experimentation that would be unacceptable to a politically entrenched and financially strong middle class.

[3] J. Gruen, *The New Bohemia* (New York: Grosset & Dunlap, Inc., 1966), p. 59.

Many designers reject the idea that the optimal environment, even for the disabled, has a single static form. Architect Raymond Studer advocates *servo-environmental systems,* which respond to changes in behavioral input. He feels that design problems phrased in terms of buildings, schools, houses, and neighborhoods obscure dynamic processes that will change over time.[4] James Marston Fitch has described a school environment that rejects day-long environmental norms—the "ideal" temperature of 72 degrees, 50 percent humidity, 60-foot lamberts at desk top, and 45 decibels of sound. A child needs less heat in the afternoon than in the morning, more oxygen and less humidity by the end of the day, as well as greater sound levels in the afternoon than in the morning. Fitch cites the example of hospitals that have created totally new environments to enhance therapy, rooms that are therapeutic tools rather than containers: the hyperbaric chamber where barometric pressure and oxygen content are regulated to treat circulatory disorders and gas gangrene; metabolic surgery suites where body temperature can be reduced to slow metabolic rates before difficult surgery; the use of saturated atmospheres for serious cases of burns; artificially cooled, dry air to lighten the thermal stress on cardiac cases; and the use of electrostatic precipitation and ultraviolet radiation to produce completely sterile atmospheres for difficult respiratory ailments and prevention of cross-infection from contagious diseases.[5] Such total environments have the greatest applicability when the individual is passive, helpless, or infirm. Since he cannot look after himself or seek out and alter the environment to fit his needs, then it is necessary for others to do the job for him.

This work rests on the assumption that the needs of these specific individuals can be known and used in programming facilities. Larger questions about the place of these people in society remain unmasked and hence unanswered. A handbook of housing for the elderly will recommend bright illumination, non-skid floors, windows for looking out, and so forth. One cannot argue with these recommendations (although one can ask whether they do not apply to all people rather than just the elderly), but they miss the overriding issue of segregation or integration. A building that caters to an elderly person's need for support, visual stimulation, and privacy, but is disabling him socially is hardly an ideal solution to his problems. One can spend a lot of time researching the design of prisons without getting into the question of whether prisons as they now exist, even the best ones, do more

---

[4] Studer, *op. cit.*

[5] James Marston Fitch, "The Esthetics of Function," *Annals of the New York Academy of Sciences,* CXXVIII (1965), 706–14.

harm than good. Given the drug laws and treatment procedures that now exist, it would be a waste of time for an architect to design a building for drug addicts.

When society constructs special institutions for classes of non-persons, the idea of Utopia is not very relevant. For the most part these institutions are designed with society's interests in mind rather than the individual's. Consider the large state hospitals which, at this moment, incarcerate 700,000 men and women in North America.[6] Has an attempt been made to design these institutions from the standpoint of the patient's own needs, with respect for his way of life, his craving for privacy and refuge? The poorest institutions are designed with security, custody, and economy in mind, the best for something nebulously called therapy or rehabilitation. In no sense can a therapeutic milieu be equated with one designed to give happiness and pleasure to the inmates. Therapy implies society's goals and interests rather than the patient's. It is stipulated by law that patients must be treated humanely while receiving therapy, but the idea of changing the individual is implicit in the concept of therapy. Let us contrast the state hospitals with a designed Utopia, Storyland Park in the Pocono Mountains of Pennsylvania. Storyland is intended as a childhood imagination come true. Besides the junior fire engine, there is a Western town with a real jail where each child can be Sheriff. There are tunnels to crawl through, walls to climb, things to take apart, an absence of no-no's—in short, everything to delight and interest the child. Buildings are child-sized, with small doors and windows, tiny tables and chairs, all to the child's scale. One cannot say the same of Rockland or Pilgrim State Hospital, each located in progressive New York State and containing over 10,000 patients. Yet the point is not the number of individuals incarcerated, the shortage of nurses, the crowded wards, for as we have seen, privacy is a matter of barriers rather than square footage. It would be possible, although somewhat difficult, to design a large state hospital as a Utopia for schizophrenics, at least in the way we have been using the concept. This would require that society recognize the legitimacy of the patient's way of life. For a patient who happens to be labeled schizophrenic, it means explicit recognition that withdrawal from social intercourse is a legitimate *modus vivendi*, acceptance of the fact that some people find no place to hide in society and turn within themselves for solace. Strange mannerisms, bizarre dress, and crazy talk are all means for keeping other people at a distance. Is society willing and able to build

---

[6] On the average day in 1966, another 400,000 Americans resided in various prisons, jails, and detention centers.

institutions—asylums, refuges, communities, call them what you want—for people who want to avoid contact with others?

At first glance this is a dollars-and-cents question, whether society can afford it. I will not try to answer the question in terms of specific amounts. What society can afford to pay is largely dependent on political considerations and the felt needs of its leaders. Under John F. Kennedy there was an awareness of mental retardation, and under Lyndon B. Johnson the poor were discovered. At this moment two billion dollars a month are being spent on a war in a small Asian nation. Set in this context, the question whether society can afford to build retreats becomes meaningless. Of more relevance is the fact that American society already maintains institutions for 700,000 of these people. Would it be more or less costly to switch from the present system of custody and behavior change to one of refuge and protection from unwanted social intercourse? There can be no doubt that a refuge would be less expensive to staff, particularly if it were maintained by the inmates themselves who possessed gardens and tools for handicrafts and light industry. There would be no need for several thousand employees—gardeners, cooks, accountants, and attendants. The amount varies from state to state, but in California it costs $14 per patient per day to remain in a state mental hospital, which works out to about $5,110 per patient per year. One could construct and maintain a very nice refuge—including a private chalet for each patient—with this amount of money. The problem, then, is not the cost of the plan but society's reluctance to underwrite an institution that is basically subversive to its own values.

In mental hospital design, we see that it is possible to conceive of Utopia as a place where society's interests are served and everything operates to make a cohesive and efficient society. The individual does not learn the wrong habits because the environment has been programmed to optimize the well-being of the collective. This has something of both Skinner and Marx in it. Considered in this way, the mental hospital and the prison are behavior change mechanisms in a larger Utopia designed to benefit the full society. This contrasts with the view of Utopia as a world designed to meet the needs of the individual residents. This brings us to the notion of the individual's rights versus those of society, which is as relevant to city and regional planning as it is to forensic psychiatry. The libertarian view is that Utopia maximizes the individual's right to do as he pleases and society is a hypothetical construct composed of the sum total of individual efforts. There should be no zoning, setback, or esthetic regulations pertaining to home building, except those required by safety and/or public health. Opposed to this is the view that Utopia can operate only at the societal or even world level at which the needs of the collective, as expressed in majority will or the decisions of elected representatives, are paramount. If the citizens decree that all houses in an area must cost $25,000 or occupy lots of a certain size and shape, or fit certain styles, the individual must bow or move out. The concept of Utopia involves fundamental decisions regarding the rights of the individual vis-à-vis society, which becomes very clear when we examine the needs of the schizophrenic compared with those of society. The example is felicitous because, unlike the deviant individual who wants to become a painter, inventor, or political activist, it is almost impossible to say that the withdrawal of the schizophrenics from society contributes to the welfare of the society; in the case of the schizophrenic the issue is primarily one of civil rights and secondarily of economics.

To use another example, it requires no great imagination to program an ideal world for a drug addict. The major requirements would be place where he can obtain his drugs and then go about the business of living a full productive life. One can, of course, be concerned with the sorts of interior spaces—deep carpets, lounge chairs, music, soft lights—that will enhance the drug experience, but an American addict at this moment would settle for an unfurnished basement so long as he can have his drugs. No precise figures are available, but addicts frequently use public toilets for shooting drugs—certainly not the most attractive settings. Once an addict's need for drugs is met, then we can start making provision for other aspects of his life. His Utopia would be very different from a Synanon or Lexington or any other institution designed to help him live without drugs. In the present social climate, it may be simpler to program a drugless Synanon than to change the laws, but this does not mean that such a world is more suited to the addict's explicit needs. Instead of the present policy, which costs untold millions in theft, erratic enforcement, unsuccessful rehabilitation, and human suffering, society could choose to legitimize the addict's need for drugs, just as it might accept the schizophrenic's expressed needs for isolation and the homosexual's for liaison with people of like inclination. Society already tolerates nudists and monastics, allowing them to carry out their rituals in geographic isolation.

On the other hand, it would be a mistake to assume that the integration of special groups of people into the larger society is always desirable. A sizable number of elderly people prefer to live in segregated communities. The reasons can be manifold—to avoid school taxes or simply a desire for a more serene environment. Whatever the reasons, many people have chosen segregation to the extent of voting with their feet and dollars. Here is an excerpt from a speech by a director of a segregated adult community to a service club:

> Move to Carefree Village and live longer. It has been proven that people in retirement centers live five to ten years longer. Why stagnate yourselves living all your life in one place? Come down to Carefree Village and do the things you've always dreamed about. It will open a new way of life to you. The people there come from congestion and screaming kids. You can play horseshoes, use the sauna baths, and we have a wood shop where you men can make the things you've always dreamed about. Today I saw a dozen people on bicycles. There is a bus into town. People get out and move.

The superordinate question facing planners today is integration versus segregation. Whether one is discussing the place of the elderly in society, suburbs vis-à-vis the central city, housing for low-income groups, or the location of medical services, one is forced to weigh the needs of those people who would gain from segregation with the needs of those who would suffer from it. In the cases of the suburban bedroom communities or the instant cities, we are dealing with self-segregation, the voluntary removal of large numbers of white middle-class families from an increasingly unpleasant central city. The process thereby leaves an involuntarily segregated mass of poor people, problem families, and ethnic minorities at the city core. Some elderly people can afford the comfortable segregation of Leisure World, but others are relegated to run-down hotels and homes for the aged.

As we saw in Chapter 2, space is related to status not only in amount but also in quality. The high status individual has better space and more of it. Most attempts to equalize the situation on a limited scale are bound to fail because high status individuals also have greater mobility and will move to places where their prerogatives are respected. It is hardly surprising that people will avoid juvenile delinquency, congestion, air pollution, and welfare problems if they can. The interests of a superordinate aggregate such as the citizens of an entire city or region may be different from those of a subgroup.

Most planners are pessimistic about the chances of obtaining integration—economic as well as ethnic—through the efforts of private builders. Of the New Towns being built in this country, the vast majority will exclude poor people. If a developer decided to bring problem families into his new community, the risks of such a policy are appreciable and material, the rewards strictly intangible. Theodore Roszak believes, "Only under government direction can a real garden city be built. For perhaps only a public agency can successfully coordinate population with industry . . . and absorb the costs of setting up in the towns low income housing that wouldn't be an intolerable eyesore or a potential slum tract from the outset." [7]

Roszak implicitly takes the position that a true garden city must be a self-contained unit whose occupants work locally and whose workers reside locally in contrast to the bedroom suburb where the husbands earn their money in the city and whose working force of clerks, salesladies, and maids live elsewhere. It is reasonable to make the minimization of travel one criteria of Utopian living, but I doubt if it should be the major criterion. Many families are willing to trade commuting costs to obtain lawns, quiet, and freedom from urban problems, just as the residents of Salem or New Harmony voluntarily removed themselves from corruption.

Self-segregation has typically been a major (but not the only) ingredient of Utopianism, and in evaluating its benefits and disadvantages we need to look beyond the welfare of the segregated group. Not only must we ask how older people fare in Leisure World, we must also measure the effects of the exodus of the elderly from the larger community—what does it do to the family traditions and culture when the people most intimately acquainted with the old days are no longer around? The young unmarrieds of Los Angeles who move into age-segregated housing to obtain country club living (built incidentally by people who started out constructing segregated housing for senior citizens) are the vanguard of a trend that is likely to have important social consequences in terms of boy-meets-girl. When one discusses segregation, he must eventually deal with questions of integration. To remove mental patients from society may temporarily ease their burdens and make life simpler for their families, but what happens when it comes time to return the patient to a family and community that has adjusted to his absence? We are dealing with hierarchies of needs and interdependencies, with ecosystems rather than isolated individuals and groups. There is no situation that is ideal for everyone all of the time. This is the true meaning of Utopia as a nonplace.

[7] T. Roszak, "Life in the Instant Cities," *The Nation* (March 13, 1967), pp. 336–40.

11

Behavioral Research and

Environmental Programming

To a greater extent than perhaps any other nation, we Americans have become an "indoor" people. A large portion of our lives—working, sleeping, playing—is spent in buildings: buildings over whose design and construction we have little or no control; buildings whose physical and economic distribution are only remotely conditioned by our needs; buildings whose effect upon our health and happiness is only obscurely understood. (J. M. Fitch, *American Building*)

As a psychologist in the design fields, I write articles on hospital design for hospital administrators, on outdoor study spaces for landscape designers, on classroom seating for teachers and principals, and so on. I am less interested in the specific substance of my results, since I lack the time, facilities, and commitment to do a really extensive study of any single setting, than in demonstrating the relevance of behavior research to practitioners. The goal is to stimulate individuals in the field to undertake this research themselves. When someone comes into a situation, does research, and then leaves, barely a ripple of change appears. It is better to get the people involved in the situation to conduct the research themselves, even if the research is of inferior quality. This is one lesson of the Peace Corps experience. Although it is easier for the corpsmen to build a well or a school themselves than to get the local people to do it, if they do it themselves and leave, the situation would revert to the *status quo* quickly. Not until practitioners in the design fields and space managers become concerned with how their buildings affect people are we going to have some meaningful

155

changes taking place. When a designer or user participates in evaluation research, the situation is no longer one of an outsider coming in, telling him in a foreign language how to run his business, and leaving on the next plane.

An occupational hazard of environmental consulting is that the client receives the impression that all problems can be solved by pushing through a wall or rearranging the chairs. Things just are not that simple. Any change in the physical or organizational structure of a hospital, office, or household will require some rearrangement of other items, but there is no guarantee that any single change will produce the desired results. Frequently it is the fact of change itself that is important—shaking things up or "making it hot for them," to use Terry Southern's phrase.

More than anything else, the interest shown by management in environmental change conveys to others that experiment and innovation are encouraged and will be supported. Such changes within an organization tend to be infectious. Department heads feel that they cannot sit still when others are experimenting with new procedures and programs. A new car on the block creates some dissatisfaction among neighbors on all sides. When one man redecorates his office, others will follow. So much is written about the deterioration of environment, that we tend to overlook people's desires for beauty and harmony. A single renovation or beautification program accomplishes more by creating an awareness of the possibilities of change than as a statistical increment of beauty in a desolate or ugly world.

The contributions of social scientists to design fields are going to change over the years. Right now they will be most useful in teaching designers how to evaluate existing structures and in participating in such evaluations as a member of a research team. This means going out into windowless schools and offices, low income housing projects, and adventure playgrounds to see how the people are using the facilities and what they think of them. This will provide a good body of case studies of individual design solutions. If there is great consistency in the way that people react to certain design features or a larger architectural element, some generalization may be possible.

Considered from the standpoint of a single building, evaluation research is not very practical since the findings will come too late to be of use to the clients. However if we are dealing with a building system that will expand and change over time, then this criticism becomes invalid. A 300-bed hospital may not be constructed all at one time but rather in three increments of 100 beds each. This will make it possible to include the results from behavioral studies of the first wing into the planning and design of the second and third wings. Such a procedure was followed by Wheeler in his collaboration with an architectural firm designing college dormitories for several Indiana campuses. From the study of the first unit they derived information that modified the plans for the subsequent dormitories. The first dormitory lounge was a large open area, the usual sort of status space that impresses parents and visitors but provides limited privacy for the residents. In the second residence hall a two-level plan reduced complaints substantially. The formal lounge was divided into four areas by means of a central chimney; activity areas were located on a mezzanine.[1]

Where circumstances permit, the research team can conduct experiments within the setting. In view of the amount of money involved in large-scale renovation, these will probably be rather modest ventures. Time will also be a limitation since a structure or area should be observed over a period of years rather than weeks. In terms of priorities, it would seem that collecting the observational and survey data from existing settings would have the greatest immediate payoff.

Given our present state of ignorance, I have serious misgivings about social scientists becoming involved in the actual design of buildings. When an architect comes to me with plans for a conference room or college dormitory, I can only make the wildest guesses as to how these are going to work in practice—unless of course they are so obvious that any observer could make the same predictions. I have no special competence in predicting how customers will react to an open-plan bank or a round auditorium. All I can say is: "If you are interested in knowing about open-plan banks, build one and let me observe it, or hire me to visit open-plan banks and a few closed-plan structures for comparison purposes." Even when I advise about a building type I know well—college dormitories—I feel compelled to preface it this way: "Although we found these opinions held at 20 dormitories in California, your situation in Salt Lake City or Toronto may be different, so borrow carefully from our findings."

I feel that at this point in time, social scientists can be most useful in evaluating existing structures. It is premature to involve them in the design process unless they have had prior experience with a building type or will have sufficient time to acquire relevant data. It would be regrettable if social scientists were brought into architectural firms as status symbols, for their great potential contribution as data

---

[1] Lawrence Wheeler, *Behavioral Research for Architectural Planning and Design* (Terre Haute, Indiana: Ewing Miller, Associates, 1967).

gatherers will be lost if they become merely sources of anecdote, myth, and analogy.

The need for translating scientific findings into a form usable by practitioners exists in almost every field. Few engineers can read physics journals and few medical men can read journals of biochemistry. It would be a waste of time for architects to keep abreast of journals in psychology or sociology; few social scientists are able to do this either. The one relevant article in a hundred would have an ambiguous title: "The Effects of Proximity on Clique Structure," or "Luminosity and Color Perception." Furthermore, the practical implications of relevant findings are not always apparent. It has been shown that there are more friendships in dormitories with common washrooms than in those with private washrooms, but what does this mean to an architect who wants to design for privacy as well as for friendliness? For almost every item in a building program there is the qualification that too much of a good thing is undesirable.

The delay in using social science data in the design fields is a product of several factors. There is, for one thing, the reluctance of designers to replace their reliance on intuition, artistry, and perceptual values such as harmony, integrity, and cohesion with the jargon of a new group of self-proclaimed experts. The coalescing of individuals and professions with diverse training, viewpoint, and perceptual style requires the time for each group to become accustomed to each other and this can only occur in a nonthreatening situation. Case studies of design solutions such as buildings or parks cannot be undertaken with an attitude of finding out what is wrong with the place. This is particularly true when it comes to publishing the results of such studies. Fortunately there is some precedent in biomedical research where case studies are published without the names of the individuals. A physician describes twenty cases of sleeping sickness, the first is a woman age 54 with two children, the second a man age 38, unmarried, and so on; a public health team describes the locale of its study as "A small Kansas town of 1500 people, primarily a marketing and commercial center for the surrounding agriculture area." Community surveys typically employ pseudonyms (Middletown or Prairieville) or a general statement about "three suburban communities on the east coast." Economists and others studying business organizations do not identify a company by name in published articles. Many precedents exist for evaluating schools, office buildings, and housing projects without mentioning the individuals or companies involved and thus avoiding *ad hominem* arguments or the creation of a form of negative awards system.

Also needed is a middleman who is acquainted with the design field as well as with the social sciences to translate relevant behavioral data into terms meaningful to designers. Thomas Seabrook advocates the category of planner-sociologist in the city planning field.[2] Such a person would translate behavioral theories and facts into the range of tolerance with which the physical planner can cope. Seabrook asks of what relevance is it to know that poorer families are less mobile, more neighborhood oriented, and depend to a greater degree on their neighbors for psychological support? If one can penetrate the jargon, these data are more interesting than helpful to planners. Someone has to tease out their design implications by asking the right questions. Does the shortage of money mean that the children and parents will spend more time in the park? Does the increased leisure of the upper middle class mean a greater need for outdoor recreational spaces? Do older people and retired individuals have special needs for benches, shaded areas, and access to restroom facilities that are not included in standard park designs?

The behavioral scientist differs from the subject-matter specialist in that he is an expert on methods for obtaining information and may know little, at least at the outset, about particular settings. Let us consider the design of a library for a NASA academy. It would be desirable for the planning board to bring in a library consultant, probably a trained librarian interested and experienced in library construction, someone who is knowledgeable about the history of the field, present developments, and where things are heading. The money invested in experienced library consultants will be returned many times over in the improved efficiency of the building and actual cost savings on specific items. However, the needs of a particular agency in a specific situation are unique, so it would be hazardous to rely solely on subject-matter knowledge in designing for specific clients. What are the special needs of NASA people? What provisions can be made for storing classified materials so they can be retrieved easily? An architect can learn much from visiting libraries at West Point and the Air Force Academy as well as from talking with librarians at regional NASA sites. To tie all this material together as well as to obtain information on the specific work habits and needs of NASA personnel may take more time and effort than the architect is willing to invest. It would be wasteful to use library consultants as data gatherers, people who go out and interview NASA personnel at various sites, although this practice has been followed. A more reasonable procedure would involve delegating the task of learning the opinions and work habits of the building's prospective residents to some person trained in the social sciences. He would introduce a different perspective, the viewpoint of someone who has assisted with environmental programming in a variety of settings. Called in by NASA, he may know nothing about military librarianship—his last job might have been with a community redevelopment agency trying to unslum a salvageable district and, before that, with a state agency drawing up specifications for playgrounds. This work has taught him how to find the needs of clients and express them in such a way that they are meaningful to designers. It is the architect who translates the building program into sketches and the sketches into a three-dimensional form, but it is the behavioral scientist who feeds information into the system about the needs of the specific people involved, just as the subject-matter expert feeds in information about like buildings elsewhere and new developments in the field.

Designers need concepts that are relevant to both physical form and human behavior. Much of architecture affects people from beyond the focus of awareness. People are not sure what it is about a building or room that affects them, nor are they able to express how they feel in different surroundings. Norbitt Mintz interviewed a large number of students in three sorts of rooms—one very attractive with modern decor, the second a room of average appearance, and the third an ugly room resembling a janitor's closet in a sad state of disrepair with an exposed light bulb, torn shade, and a tin can serving as a receptacle for cigarette ashes. When he questioned the students afterwards, he found that only 29 per cent mentioned anything about the appearance of the rooms, 46 per cent mentioned that something seemed wrong in the experiment but could not say what it was, and 25 per cent reported that the experiment was "fine." [3]

Not only do people have difficulty expressing what they feel about architecture, but most of their reactions to a division of space is on an emotional rather than a rational level. This is especially true in regard to the division of space within a house rather than the shell or enclosure. Architects rely on language even though it is apparent that words may mean different things to an architect than to a client. The way an architect uses the word "cell" to describe an office may disturb a corporation executive who associates the term with prisons.

In their studies of highway experience, Appleyard and his associates believed that their first task was to develop techniques for recording, analyzing, and communicating the visual and kinesthetic sequences of

[3] Norbitt Mintz, "Effects of Aesthetic Surroundings," *Journal of Psychology,* XLI (1956), 459–66.

highway travel. Without such techniques, it is difficult to express or refine design alternatives short of building full-scale roads. Sensing the inadequacies of photographic recording for detailed analysis of visual experience, they have developed an intriguing system analogous to the music notations used by composers in which the road becomes a spatial and kinesthetic rhythmic experience—a symphony.[4] Recently there have been attempts to develop techniques for studying the subjective connotations of structures as well as their objective dimensions. One such technique is the semantic differential developed by Charles Osgood at the University of Illinois in which concepts are rated along various scales, good to bad, strong to weak, active to passive, and so forth.[5] The same object may have vastly different connotations to different people—a hammer is a toy to a child and a tool to his father; a slum neighborhood can mean security and warmth to a child growing up there and a social problem to a city planner. One study was aimed specifically at exploring how architects use the concept of space. Architects speak of "interesting spaces" and "vital spaces," but laymen use the term to refer to a void or absence of something. Architecture students saw space as more valuable, active, and more potent than did the liberal arts students.[6] Such techniques can help us to clarify and to understand people's reactions to their surroundings. Most present architectural criticism has been written by highly literate and sensitive individuals who visit buildings for short periods and whose reactions may be unrepresentative of the building's inhabitants. Another solution is to increase the sensitivity and correct the visual and emotional blindness of people so that they can present their needs and feelings in a form that others can understand and appreciate. This may require considerable effort, and the task is being made more difficult by electronic technology, which leaves little room for human experience and meaningful social intercourse.

METHODS FOR GATHERING DATA

Laboratory experiments have generally yielded discouraging results when it comes to evaluating environmental effects on human perfor-

[4] Donald Appleyard, Kevin Lynch, and J. R. Myer, *The View from the Road* (Cambridge, Mass.: M.I.T. Press, 1964).

[5] Charles E. Osgood, G. Suci, and P. Tannenbaum, *The Measurement of Meaning* (Urbana: University of Illinois Press, 1957).

[6] Robert Sommer, "The Significance of Space," *AIA Journal* (May 1965), pp. 63–65.

mance. There are extremes of heat, cold, and humidity that have an obvious effect on behavior, but these are rarely the concern of designers interested in the normal range of sensory stimulation. Edward Thorndike conducted an elaborate series of tests for the New York State Commission on Ventilation on the efficiency of student performance under various conditions of temperature, humidity, and air movement. The tasks included laboratory exercises in naming colors and canceling digits as well as school exercises in arithmetic, English composition, and typing. Environmental conditions ranged from those that, at the time, were considered optimal (68 degrees, 50 per cent relative humidity, and 45 feet per person per minute of outside air) to those that were regarded as very unfavorable (86 degrees, 80 per cent relative humidity, and no circulation or change of air). The authors concluded:

> With the forms of work and lengths of period used, we find that when an individual is urged to do his best he does as much, and does it as well, and improves as rapidly in a hot, humid, sterile, and stagnant air condition as in an optimum condition. . . . We find further that when an individual is given work to do that is of no interest or value to him and is deprived even of the means of telling how well he does it, and is in other ways tempted to relax standards and do work of poor quality, he still shows no inferiority in the quality of the product. . . . Finally we find that when an individual is left to his own choice as to whether he shall do mental work or read stories, rest, talk, or sleep, he does as much work per hour when the temperature is 75 degrees as when it is 68 degrees.[7]

Productivity in the laboratory tends to remain constant regardless of environment. When conditions are unfavorable, the subject works harder to compensate for his handicaps. Many effects of a noxious environment are insidious and reveal themselves over the long run rather than immediately. On the other hand, it is true that symphonies have been created in basements, inventions made in garages, and masterpieces painted in unheated garrets. Whether these heroes are able to triumph because of the challenge of adversity or in spite of it is only part of the answer. We must also know how the vast majority of ordinary mortals perform in different environments. I can read a novel (but not a technical book) with the phonograph playing, but someone else will react differently.

If a ten-year-old child in New York can survive the crowding, noise, crime, and litter, it is unlikely that rearranging the chairs in his class-

---

[7] Edward L. Thorndike, W. A. McCall, and J. C. Chapman, "Ventilation in Relation to Mental Work," *Teachers College Contributions to Education*, LXXVIII (1916), 82.

room will have a significant effect on how much he learns if he wants to. A small desk or obnoxious roommate in a college dormitory is not going to lower a student's grades if he can go eleswhere to study. It will change his behavior, increasing the amount of study outside the room, but this is not a "hard performance variable" like grade point average. In the classroom experiments discussed in Chapter 7, the escape behaviors could be attributed to room environment, but there was no difference in class grades between the sections. At Rensselaer Polytechnic Institute an experimental classroom has been developed whose lighting, colored surfaces, seating types, and projection display surfaces can all be altered systematically. After several years of research, the authors admit that the question "How well does this environment perform in supporting learning?" has not been answered.[8]

Let me pose a conundrum that I think will elucidate some of the important but hidden issues in the criterion problem.

We have two chairs in a classroom, Type A and Type B, and whenever a student is given a choice, he sits in Type A. The result is that Type A chairs are occupied first and Type B remain empty when there are surplus chairs in the room. However, when there are only as many chairs as there are pupils, or students must sit in assigned places without regard to chair type, we find no difference in examination scores between students sitting in A and B chairs.

What does this mean? Does the lack of difference in examination scores mean that a school board can purchase either chair or the cheaper of the two in good conscience, that is, with the realization that the amount of learning taking place will be unaffected by their decision? I do not accept this view, and I will try to explain why. For one thing, it overlooks the totalitarian nature of institutional experience. If a house builder constructs two models, A and B, and nobody buys B, the question of whether he builds both A and B is academic. In the free market situation, he does not build anything that people will not buy. However, a school, library, or hospital board, corporation committee, or any other institutional client does not have to worry about the vagaries of the market place. If they construct small classrooms, two-man offices, and four-bed hospital rooms, they will be used and, in terms of performance criteria, probably will be just as effective as single rooms or three-man rooms. Institutional arrangements place people in situations they would not otherwise choose. We can cut the Gordian knot by making the realization of individual

[8] A. Green, "Architectural Research and the Learning Environment" (Paper presented at the Second National Conference on Architectural Psychology, Park City, Utah, 1966).

choice and satisfaction as values in their own right. If people say they like something or show by their behavior that they prefer it, this should be a value fed into the design process even though it cannot be proven that this makes a difference on a profit-and-loss statement or an academic record. Many performance criteria deal with only a single aspect of a multigoal organization. The encouragement of academic achievement is one objective of a good classroom teacher, but she also strives for personal growth, maturity, and self-direction on the part of her pupils. I am not saying that performance criteria such as profit-and-loss, days-in-hospital, or grades should be discarded. When a measure fits only a single dimension of a situation, the solution is not to reject all measurement, but to develop measures for the other aspects. Single item evaluation tends to encourage *criterion-directed performance*, which neglects important but unmeasured aspects of program success.

In a changing world it seems reasonable to establish *variety* and *flexibility* as important goals in a building program. I do not propose substituting them for harmony, unity, balance, rhythm, excitement, or the other traditional design values. Both variety and flexibility inherently increase the range of individual choice. A necessary corollary of these two values is that we must establish institutional arrangements—rules, procedures, and personnel practices—that enable individuals to exploit the variety and possibilities for flexibility in their environment. By *variety* I mean a multiplicity of settings and spaces a person can select to suit his individual needs. On my campus there is a policy regarding dormitory construction that no new residence hall complex should be identical with an existing one. The goal is to increase the range of choices available to students at the beginning of the term. The same principle can be applied to other design elements; rather than installing benches of one kind or size in parks and recreation areas, it is preferable to vary one's purchases and arrangements. *Flexibility* is expressed in such terms as multipurpose, multiuse, and convertible spaces. With rapidly changing technology and the inability to predict institutional practices even five years ahead, its importance seems obvious. It is closely tied in with *personalization* since it permits a man to adapt a setting to his unique needs.

THE HAWTHORNE MYTH

Perhaps the least understood and most maligned study in the history of the social sciences was the research into worker productivity con-

ducted at Western Electric Company. Many people have heard
Hawthorne effect or the way that production rose as working conditions
improved.[9] However, when some of the changes were reversed, production continued to rise. This has been interpreted to mean that environment did not make any difference, it was all a placebo effect—
like getting a reaction to a sugar pill. However, what the Western
Electric study showed conclusively was that environment did make a
difference. Almost every change in environmental conditions had its
effect on the workers and, often, on their production. The study also
demonstrated that there is no simple relationship between single environmental elements and complex human behavior. The effects of
environmental changes are mediated by individual needs and group
processes. The worker does not react to improved lighting or a coffee
break as the rat does to the lever in his cage that brings him a food
pellet. In an atmosphere of trust and understanding, he accepts environmental changes as indications that management is interested in
his welfare. In an atmosphere of distrust and hostility, he wonders
how management hopes to exploit him by changing his working conditions; he looks upon environmental programming as manipulation.
Behavior produced by a sugar pill is just as real and observable as
behavior produced by amphetamine. Just as some people are made
sleepy by pep pills and the magnitude of their reaction is influenced
by the presence or absence of other people, so changes in man's internal environment are not simple conditioned reflexes in which A
automatically produces B.

Studies of schools, hospitals, prisons, and slums have shown that it
is nearly impossible to isolate the specific factors responsible for a
given outcome. Neither can we tell precisely why one city can support
a major league team and another cannot, or why Topeka, Kansas, became a world-renowned center of psychiatry, but Wichita, which is a
much larger city, did not, or why one town can pass a large school bond
issue that is defeated in an adjacent city. There is no single factor that
can explain any of these phenomena. Frequently it appears that the
reason is connected with the town's self-image as a sports capital or a
cultural center or a good business town. The citizens then support the
programs that fit the town's image. San Franciscans believe themselves
to be cosmopolitan and are therefore willing to tolerate toplessness
and gay bars; the citizens of Green Bay accept with joy or resignation
the annual fall football madness. An image that is believed becomes
a self-fulfilling prophecy. The image of a city as a bad business town

[9] F. J. Roethlisberger and W. J. Dickson, *Management and the Worker* (Cambridge, Mass.: Harvard University Press, 1939).

can doom that city, and the stereotype of a neighborhood as good or bad will raise or lower real estate values. Any attempt to trace the origin of these beliefs will produce a score of causal agents, major as well as minor. The mechanisms involved in this process are similar to the Hawthorne effect. People who are concerned with solutions to particular problems are less concerned with how something works than the fact that it works. A recent review of programs for geriatric patients includes these comments: ". . . whether by a Hawthorne effect or by the specific action of the milieu program on the staff or patients, most of these programs have succeeded in raising the functioning level of their recipients in a measurable manner," [10] and "Almost any type of facility works with older brain-damaged patients. The main thing is stimulation from the environment and, of course, a radical change in attitude on the part of personnel."

The methods of the biological sciences, particularly animal biology and ecology, which rely heavily upon observation and field experimentation over long periods, seem more applicable to the design fields than the single variable laboratory experiments characteristic of physics and chemistry. A designer would profit more from training in the techniques of systematic observation than in the empty rituals included under the category of experimental design. It is extremely difficult if not impossible to execute a rigorous experiment that deals with important relationships under natural conditions. Experiments in the field are replete with unanticipated variables and *post hoc* explanations. It is unlikely that the use of laboratory models in teaching students will increase the number of field experiments or improve their quality, since the techniques necessary to undertake a good field study differ radically from those of a laboratory. For one thing the field investigator must be extremely sensitive to the structure of the environment, the important processes that are taking place, the people with whom he works, the administrative procedures that must be followed. In the classroom evaluation studies described earlier, the administrative arrangements took more time and effort than the research itself. A study in a public school requires the permission of individual teachers, the school principal and his assistants, the local school board, the county superintendent of schools and his assistants, as well as the approval and cooperation of students and parents. If any single step is omitted and some key person is not consulted, the affair can turn into a debacle. A recent article describes a study that had been cleared with all the important names on the official school hierarchy, but

[10] M. Powell Lawton, "Planning a Building for the Mentally Impaired Aged," mimeo., 1965.

the investigator forgot to contact several assistants to key people (one was out of town during the orientation session, and the other was away on a two-year leave), and, to the investigator's dismay, these assistants were the ones responsible for interpreting headquarters' policy to individual schools. Field studies are not for the soft-hearted or the administratively ignorant, they are far more complex from the standpoint of human relationships and sensitivity to social structure than laboratory studies. Occasionally an investigator finds a situation where a high-ranking official in a large operation becomes interested in behavioral studies and gives them his enthusiastic support. This was the case in the studies by Wells of the new office building of the Cooperative Insurance Company in Manchester.[11] It would have been impossible to undertake individual interviews and systematic observational studies without management's full cooperation. One cannot undertake creative environmental experimentation without the support and interest of those who are administratively responsible for the environment.

None of these methods can be applied arbitrarily. One has to learn when, where, and how to gain information. This requires a feeling for the nature of the setting and the people in it. One does not use a printed questionnaire with migrant workers, geriatric patients, or ghetto children. On the other hand, the questionnaire is a most efficient and appropriate tool for college students accustomed to written examinations and who may indeed be troubled by a personal interview that requires direct confrontation with an older person—a novel experience for many of them! With children I would choose direct observation in situations where many options are available, supplemented by interviews (both individual and group) after the observations had continued for some time. With migrant workers the use of participant observation would seem appropriate provided the researcher spoke the workers' language. Thus far we have said little about participant observation where the observer shares the daily lives of the people under study, observing things that happen, listening to what is said, and questioning people over some length of time. The method produces data that are often strikingly different from those obtained through interview or casual observation methods. A designer or some member of his staff might live in a migrant workers' camp or accompany hospital attendants through their daily routine for a few days. As an insider he sees, hears, smells, and feels things to which the general public or infrequent visitors are not privy. Spending time in a setting allows him to gain the confidence and learn the private language of

[11] Brian W. P. Wells, "The Psycho-Social Influence of Building Environment," *Building Science,* I (1965), 153–65.

the participants. He is able to question people about matters that he has observed directly (the toilet facilities in the camp or the temperature in the building on an extremely hot day) rather than employ abstract questions about heating, lighting, and ventilation. Becker and Geer believe that participant observation is most useful when a situation or institution is in a state of change. Living and working in the situation will assist the researcher in distinguishing between reactions to the present situation, memories of the past, and hopes for the future.[12]

The expense of building mock-ups and the need to evaluate building systems before they are opened to the public has created an interest in various simulation techniques ranging from wide-screen photography in assessing reactions to the cityscape to hypnosis. Aaronson has been using hypnotic induction to learn the effects of color and sound on mood, the way a person behaves when the world is lacking in depth, or when he is four feet tall. All these conditions exert a powerful influence on the way a person perceives and behaves. When the hypnotic suggestion was made to a subject that he had diminished in size, he responded by seeing everything as if it were twice as far away as usual. Events and objects took on a dreamlike character and things seemed to be moving faster than they were. He became withdrawn and apathetic and felt isolated, sleepy, and without interest. When the hypnotic set of his diminished size was removed, he felt pleased and seemed normal except for his feeling that everything looked smaller. He described the world as toylike and was much impressed with how much prettier and daintier everybody and everything looked.[13]

There is no single best method—questionnaire, interview, simulation, or experiment—for studying man's adaptations to his environment. One chooses methods to suit the problem and the people and not vice versa. These methods are generally complementary rather than mutually exclusive. One would not only interview office workers and managers, he might also work alongside them at a desk for a few weeks, observe who drinks coffee with whom and to which desk people go when they want to borrow things, and he might also examine various artifacts such as interoffice mail envelopes, which would show communication patterns within the office.

There are important ethical questions about the user's role and participation in environmental experimentation. The whole matter

[12] Howard S. Becker and Blanche Geer, "Participant Observation and Interviewing: A Comparison," *Human Organization*, XVI (1957), 28–32.

[13] Bernard S. Aaronson, "Lilliput and Brobdignag—Self and World," *American Journal of Clinical Hypnosis*, X (1968), 160–66.

of experimentation with human subjects is receiving long-needed critical attention from medical and behavioral researchers as well as lawyers and legislators. The need for strict surveillance in cases involving radiation hazards and pesticides is clear enough. The situation becomes murky in cases of sonic booms and crowded beaches, annoyances rather than dangers. Most of the building evaluation work discussed in preceding chapters did not involve serious risks to anyone's health or livelihood. However, one can still imagine a lawsuit brought by a parent who maintained that his son failed in school because he had been placed in a six-man dormitory room to fit an experimental plan devised by college authorities to evaluate the effects of room size upon study habits. To determine the justification of his complaint, one would have to know whether the student or his parents had protested his being assigned to a six-man room, whether there was a decline in his school work that seemed related to his study situation, and whether the college authorities had made some attempt to ensure that participants in the study would not suffer as a result of the room assignments. I do not feel it is immoral to assign students to facilities that are presently being used on hundreds of campuses in order to learn how they work in practice. On the contrary, it seems immoral to build and use dormitories without making some systematic attempt to evaluate their effectiveness.

Administrative practices and informal understandings within an organization imprint themselves upon people until they accept them without question. The evidence from perceptual experiments is consistent in finding that familiarity does not breed contempt, but rather increased liking. This can be seen as an adaptive reaction in the human organism to permit it to adjust to a multitude of conditions. Not only will people adapt to crowding, noise, and traffic in the city, they will find it difficult to live in any other environment. Zajonc and Harrison have studied the connection between exposure and preference. In one study people were shown a series of photographs of faces —some faces were exposed once, some twice, some ten times, some 25 times. Afterwards it was found that the more a face had been shown to a person, the more he liked it. The same result was obtained when Chinese characters were used as stimuli. The more a Chinese character was exposed, the more likely did people feel that it stood for an attractive word or something they would like.[14]

Studies like this can tell us something about the dynamics of habitu-

[14] Robert B. Zajonc, "The Attitudinal Effects of Mere Exposure," *Journal of Personality and Social Psychology*, monograph supplement, IX (1968), 1–27. Also see A. A. Harrison, "Response Competition and Attitude Change as a Function of Repeated Stimulus Exposure" (Ph.D. thesis, University of Michigan, 1967).

ation and environmental preference. There are many other perceptual experiments dealing with illusions[15] and the effects of human needs on perception[16] that are relevant to spatial behavior. However it is important that architects guard themselves against *perceptual reductionism*. This attitude has all the weaknesses of the biological reductionism of Ardrey[17] and others who see in man's spatial behavior the clear expression of instinctual drives. On a technical level, the distinction here is one of analogy and homology. Behavior that is similar in appearance between species may be triggered by entirely different mechanisms. A person's behavior is affected by how he perceives the world as well as his biological makeup but both are overlaid and shaped through learning. Environmental adaptations are too complex and multidetermined to be reduced either to instincts or perceptual laws.

Finally we come to the question of applying the results of these studies. Any building must meet the diverse needs of occupants whose interests frequently conflict. A wife's need for cooking space will compete with TV space and play area for the children. A public building that serves numerous client groups will have an even larger number of competing demands made upon it. One cannot design a college dormitory solely for individual privacy since this is also the students' main social area. A store must serve the needs of shoppers, clerks, and store detectives. Some engineers and scientists have tried to side-step this problem by substituting harmony, coherence, or efficiency as the ultimate criterion of a design solution. A recent review states:

> Man is the most unreliable part of the man-machine-environment complex with which the system engineer deals. For the time being, he is tolerated in the system because he is either cheaper or has some skill which no machine has. Eventually he will be displaced by a more reliable component. This will not be so bad so long as some people remain in the system, but at last the day will come when even the system engineer will be replaced by a superior robot designer. At that stage, society will have developed a set of design values to replace the more old-fashioned and inefficient human values.[18]

[15] A. Ames, "Visual Perception and the Rotating Trapezoidal Window," *Psychological Monographs*, No. 324 (1951).

[16] Charles M. Solley and Gardner Murphy, *Development of the Perceptual World* (New York: Basic Books, Inc., Publishers, 1960).

[17] Robert Ardrey, *The Territorial Imperative* (New York: Atheneum Publishers, 1966).

[18] Luigi Petrullo, review of *The New Utopians*, in *Contemporary Psychology*, XII (1967), 165.

One can design a system in which machines work efficiently to serve other machines, prisons that serve the short-term interests of people outside, and universities that serve the needs of researchers rather than students. One outcome is as feasible as any other. A design problem is a value problem: whose interests are to be served.

It is difficult for the ordinary citizen to get a handle on the larger environmental problems of pollution, pesticides, and congestion where the causes are complex, relationships between cause and effect obscure, effects insidious, and cures expensive. Most of the time we are spectators at a grand tragedy wondering if we can last through the final act. The minor spaces around us, our bedrooms, offices, schools, and streets bring problems of another, more manageable magnitude. A man's office can be a stimulating, esthetically pleasing, and highly personal place, or it can be a cold, impersonal, and bureaucratic area that belongs to the company through its surrogates, the custodians. A conference room can bring people together or it can prevent them from hearing and seeing one another, diminish their interest in the proceedings, and create cliques. Privacy for Americans is mainly a matter of visual protection against other people, but open plan housing is moving in the opposite direction. The bank manager may tell a customer that they cannot be overheard as they talk in the center of a large office, but the customer will not feel comfortable, nor will the manager believe that the space is really his unless he can personalize it in some way. The myth of infinite plasticity must be discarded in the design of minor spaces, too. The price paid in adapting to uncongenial environments may be difficult to estimate in money, sickness, inefficiency, and turnover, but it is too high if we can design congenial environments for the same money or less. There is a lesson to be learned when executives put calendars and charts on the backs of glass doors, college students choose old barracks over modern dormitories, and Sylvia Ashton-Warner, the talented teacher of Maori children, prefers her dilapidated prefab to the elegant glass castle where the teachers are concerned with proper coathooks and preventing the chairs from scraping the new floor. People like spaces they can call their own and make over; they reject an alien environment that is built according to detailed square footage allocations for a standard model of impersonal humanity in the most durable and antiseptic condition. The man of tomorrow whose capacity to respond to the environment is reduced, may be excused from this lesson, but we are not.

The situation in the agricultural fields is instructive. Engineers and agricultural economists believe that if the production of a crop cannot be mechanized, the crop will eventually disappear. Since ordinary tomatoes cannot withstand the rough treatment of mechanical harvesting in which the fruit is shaken from the vine and placed in large bins, a new breed of tomato has been developed. It has a tough skin, and the fruit ripens at the same time so a machine can make a single run through a field. Experiments are underway to give a cube shape so it can be stored easily. "Tomatoes" are being harvested mechanically but they are a different fruit from the ones we have known. "Man" of the future, barring a nuclear holocaust, will adapt to hydrocarbons in the air, detergents in the water, crime in the streets, and crowded recreational areas. Good design becomes a meaningless tautology if we consider that man will be reshaped to fit whatever environment he creates. The long-range question is not so much what sort of environment we want, but what sort of man we want.

Index